The Ha

MW00831802

Discovering Your Joy, Power, and
Freedom Through Movement

The Hart Method

Discovering Your Joy, Power, and Freedom Through Movement

Armando Hart

YouSpeakIt
PUBLISHING
*The Easy Way
to Get Your Book
Done Right* ™
www.YouSpeakItPublishing.com

Copyright © 2017 Armando Hart

All rights reserved. No part of this book may be reproduced or transmitted in any form or by any means without written permission of the publisher, except in the case of brief quotations embodied in critical articles and reviews.

This material has been written and published solely for educational purposes. The author and the publisher shall have neither liability nor responsibility to any person or entity with respect to any loss, damage, or injury caused or alleged to be caused directly or indirectly by the information contained in this book.

The author of this book does not dispense medical advice or prescribe the use of any technique as a form of treatment for physical, emotional, or medical problems without the advice of a physician, either directly or indirectly. The intent of the author is only to offer information of a general nature to help the reader in the quest for well-being. In the event the reader uses any of the information in this book for self or others, which is a constitutional right, the author and the publisher assume no responsibility for the actions of the reader.

Statements made in this book have not been evaluated by the Food and Drug Administration. This book and its contents are not intended to diagnose, treat, or cure any infection, injury, or illness, or prevent any disease. Results vary and each person's experience is unique.

Statements made and opinions expressed in this publication are those of the author and do not necessarily reflect the views of the publisher or indicate an endorsement by the publisher.

Front cover photo by: Rodrigo Roque IV
Back cover photo by: Starla Fortunato

ISBN: 978-1-945446-36-8

Chances are that all the books you've read were dedicated to a person you didn't know. Every word on this book was written with you in my heart, mind, and body.

This one's for you.

Acknowledgments

There have been so many people who have been put in my path to help bring this book to life. To all my mentors, coaches, trainers, teachers, friends, and family: I am grateful for your help and encouragement.

To the mentors of my youth, especially Coach Irvin and Coach Cablayan: thank you for understanding my situation and supporting me in spite of my limitations.

Thank you, Coach Petkovic, for my *rocket start*.

And thank you, Coaches Cosme Rodriquez and Elbert Pratt, for connecting me to my roots.

Thank you, Larry Silva and Tom Tellez, for helping me to *put my foot down*.

To my parents, Diego and Alicia, and to my beautiful wife, Yve: you have made me a better man. Thank you.

To my son, Raya: Thank you for making me a better father.

Thank you to the YouSpeakIt support team.

Thank you to my life, for giving me exactly what I needed to share the message within this book.

Contents

Introduction

We are all born with a natural potential that can spark creativity, vision, energy, and joy. However, what you do with this potential is up to you. Children instinctively draw upon it, but as you age, you must make a conscious choice:

Will you carry your potential with you and use it?

Will you cut off your potential, ignore it, and get absorbed in your head instead?

Too many of us make the second choice. My objective for writing this book is to help you reignite the spark of potential within you so that you can reconnect with your power. The message I want to share is that this natural essence is still within you and connecting to it can change your life in amazing ways.

Look around you. There are so many paths open to you.

Why not live and create from the best possible path available?

We all inherently desire harmony, freedom, connection, expansion, and joy—virtues that were once naturally embodied by all of us as children. My own journey started many years ago—forty-two years to be exact—

but I'll fast-forward to the point in my life when I reached a critical crossroads.

I had two choices:

- I could continue in my high school teaching profession in which I taught Spanish and the only thing I looked forward to was the dismissal bell on Fridays.

- I could pursue my childhood dreams, passions, and aspirations involving physical movement and human potential.

After going into a deep meditative state asking for guidance, I heard a voice in my head that told me to go get a car wash.

Wow, God, you are pretty clever, I said to myself, smiling.

I listened to the advice and drove over to the nearest car wash. I paid for my wash and sat down. I found myself sitting right next to Misty May-Treanor, two-time Olympic gold medalist in beach volleyball.

Well, this is interesting, I thought.

Misty and I had met before; we had been classmates in college. We talked as we waited for our cars. After I expressed my passion for training others, she asked for my help.

When Misty suffered a traumatic injury—a rupture of her Achilles tendon—on the show *Dancing with the Stars*, she almost retired from volleyball. At this point, Misty invited me to become part of her training team and I started to work with her using *The Hart Method*, a method that was born from my own traumatic Olympic experience—which I will share with you later in this book.

Misty went on to win her third Olympic gold medal and is now an icon in the sport of beach volleyball. She even made it to the Wheaties box! I'm eternally grateful to Misty for giving me the opportunity to work with her and to be a witness to her success. I'm so glad that I took that trip to the car wash!

I'm sure you are wondering: *Where did that voice come from and how were you able to hear it?*

In that moment of contemplation, I believe I had connected with myself in such a deep way that the answer was given effortlessly. Before that day, I was trying and searching for solutions but getting nowhere because there was a disconnection between my head and body. That moment was a turning point in my life. It gave me a new understanding that has helped me many times.

Have you ever felt like you were in a place where everything happened for you—effortlessly?

It's magical, right?

Well, what if I told you that it's completely natural?

It is your birthright to embody this essence, to exist in this place where all your needs are met. And even beyond that, you may surpass your own expectations. I call this being in the *field of possibilities*. There is no special formula or secret to get you into this zone. You have already been there — you were born there — and I'm only here to remind your body and your mind to remember. After reading this book and learning about The Hart Method, I hope you will understand that you can remind yourself with a simple shift in body movement.

What do you need in order to do this?

Well, when you awaken every morning, can you sense your body, your breath, and your awareness?

What if I told you that's all you need to get back in the game?

It's time to get back to the field of possibilities.

As a child living in this field of possibilities, I dreamed of making a difference in this world. Ultimately, this dream gave birth to The Hart Method. The method is focused on these eight maxims:

1. Ground
2. Gravity
3. Integrity
4. Joy
5. Harmony
6. Freedom
7. Now
8. Action

We are naturally an embodiment of these virtues and they directly affect how we move our bodies and live our lives. Children live according to these elements without trying. They naturally have the power to create from a space of nothingness. In their world, there is no past and no future. Children naturally magnetize their needs — they draw what they need toward them — and they are masters at being expressive with their emotions without being defined by them.

Adults, however, need to constantly redirect themselves to stay connected to their natural essence. The Hart Method is designed to help. Using this method myself has had a huge impact on my life. I now feel that I have a way to bring powerful change to the individual lives of others. For me, it is the realization of a life-long dream.

In this book, you will read how The Hart Method uses a subtle but powerful shift in physical movement to help people to reconnect with this lost and forgotten potential. Once my body felt the shift, my life started to change. My world started to change. And when my personal world changed, the actual world changed as well.

Your outer world is a reflection of your inner world. We are like mirrors; the world responds to what it sees in us. My body holds untapped potential that I'm still learning more about every day. I'm excited for the future, but I keep my awareness in this moment. I'm fully in this moment with you right now.

Your body possesses natural genius and it is just waiting for you to come into harmony with it. Get your power back. Come back to yourself. You are capable of reprogramming yourself and in the process, you can connect to something greater. You can experience true harmony of body and mind. You can experience true freedom and joy. Your own outcome will be determined by your connection. And when you transcend, the world will transcend as well.

Don't set out to change the world; you will soon be overwhelmed by the task. Instead, as you awaken in the morning, know that you can *be* the change. And the change is always available for you because it can be accessed by the movement of your own body.

In the middle of writing this book, my father passed away. At his memorial service, I spoke about a law that we all know: the law of gravity. What goes up must come down.

But I talked about it from another perspective: *What goes down must come up.*

My father's ultimate fear was death. However, for a flower to grow, there must be a seed that goes down into the earth. For the baby to walk, it must fall. In my case, my life expanded only after collapsing in agony. I believe that a gift can be found for all of us as we are going down. We only need to be aware to see it.

Going down will always give you a new opportunity to ascend and transcend into a new reality. A dancer needs an even platform to perform. A trampoline performer goes higher if his fall is longer and more aware. Your life will become a masterpiece once you master the art of the fall. What goes down must come up.

I want you to read my book with an open mind, with an open heart, and with imagination. Imagine your own possibilities. Imagine your goals and do your best to embody them. Embody what you are imagining. Feel it in your body and your breath. Be open to the ideas and the inspirations that come. Be like a child: wide-eyed and full of wonder.

Having an intention along with a vision is key, but put your focus and awareness on the process and not on the outcome. Only then can fulfillment come. Putting your focus on the outcome will likely cost you the price of disconnecting from your body, from the present, and from the journey.

I now live in the field of possibilities, but I'm continually challenged. I must continually be aware so I don't slip back to the sidelines. I must practice every day so I can remain in this place. Life will be life, after all, and challenges always come. It's up to us to navigate through the challenges.

I have a routine in the morning in which I do simple movements for about three minutes, synchronizing body and breath. Then I sink into a feeling of gratitude to connect with what I am grateful for. I finish with dancing, moving my body, feeling good, and imagining my dreams coming true.

Every day is an opportunity, an opportunity that you have to feel good. Even when hard times come, remain present and know that you have the power to minimize difficulties by resisting attachment to those dark spaces. Be present and don't allow yourself to get stuck in there. These hard times can be powerful or destructive, depending on your approach. Making one simple physical movement can reignite your joy.

It isn't complicated. All you need to do is remember so you can help the body remember. When your mind reconnects with your body, you will feel like a light bulb is turning on.

You will feel your body saying: *Wow, I remember this. This feels so good.*

You can experience harmony again, and the joy that you were meant to feel. You can give birth to new possibilities by rewiring yourself and connecting back to your essence. There is nothing new you need to get. It's all right here. The ground is right beneath you, and your body is right there with you. You have all the tools available, right here, right now.

Ignite your joy.

CHAPTER ONE

Remember the Joy

THE JOY OF HAVING DREAMS AND ASPIRATIONS

The natural essence of your potential is born within you.

As a baby, you breathed with your whole body just as you were designed to. You developed and grew, and through movement, you naturally gained coordination and strength. When you started to walk, you were possessed with a natural determination to walk. You tried to step forward with your newly formed legs and probably fell down often.

Did your parents yell at you with anger when you fell?

Of course not. Parents are excited to watch their children learning to walk. New toddlers don't get down on themselves when they fall; they just try again. If you watch them, you can also see that they are completely engrossed in what they are doing. It is part of our natural essence to be present in the moment this way.

The influence of this natural essence is not only evident in a child's physical development. It is this same natural essence that enables you to have desires and dreams and to strive for goals of all kinds; it is what enables you to aspire to become something more than what you are.

It all begins with wanting to walk. It begins with the desire to take that first step.

I can remember what it felt like when I started to have that desire. It is an internal memory that I can still find within me. In that moment, there was nothing outside of me determining how I acted or how I behaved. There was no outside influence directing my behavior, just my own internal self—my natural essence. I was totally present within my body and my spirit.

I frequently go back to that time in my life so that I can remember that state of being. We are all born with this natural essence and it is the source of our power. This natural essence begins with the pure essence of physical movement. As young children, we moved through the world with the joy that comes from living in our natural essence. You and I had big dreams and aspired to make them come true.

What happened to us?

The Dreams I Had as a Little Boy

I remember watching Carl Lewis run in the 1984 Olympics and witnessing the joy that he brought to so many people.

I was still young enough at that point to be able to access my natural essence so I could create powerful dreams and aspirations. While watching Carl Lewis as a little boy, two dreams were born inside me:

- I wanted to be the fastest man in the world.
- I wanted to bring joy to people.

Those two dreams that were born in that moment were to become key parts of my childhood, and would be carried with me into adulthood.

To become the fastest man in the world, I needed to fulfill my potential physically. The goals of being a proponent of change and touching people's lives were destined to have many different facets in my life, as you will see.

Running for My People

My parents came from a little town called La Angostura in Michoacán, Mexico. They immigrated to America in 1972. In La Angostura, there was a tradition of festivities that revolved around foot races. My father and I went back to visit the town when I was a little boy. Together, we watched two men run against each other. I remember sitting on top of my father's shoulders watching the town explode in joy when their local runner won.

I wanted to do that!

When my family discovered that I had speed, they threw me into the underground circuit of foot races at only eleven years of age.

Being immersed in running prize foot races wasn't like Carl Lewis running at the Olympics. It wasn't fulfilling my dream of being the fastest man in the world. No, prize running was a different world, a different culture, but there was such joy in it—for me as well as for the people watching.

I saw how running could bring a sense of unity and joy for others and it was inspiring to me. I raced in this underground world until my early thirties, winning prize money and helping other people—*my people*, I called them—win money. It was common for my people to go back to their little town in Mexico and party their winnings away at the annual *fiestas*. Through my running, I brought many people joy—and it was a joy for me as well. In fact, my running motion was so joyful and effortless that sometimes, spectators wondered if I was even trying.

Where did this effortless joy and movement come from?

- Competition was a motivating factor, but it wasn't at the root of my joy.

- Winning money for others and helping them live a better life was good, but it wasn't what brought me true pleasure.

- It felt like I was magnetically attracting everything I needed in life through my movements. Without trying or forcing, all my needs were met and my body, mind, and dreams were in complete harmony.

- The joy and harmony were ignited by the natural movements of my body.

The Impact of Our Beliefs

Shortly after I started to run these one-on-one races, there was a large migration of people from my village in Mexico to Los Angeles. Continuing the tradition of racing made them feel at home — and I was *their* runner. Their excitement grew once they found out about my ability to consistently win these races.

My father and I had a close relationship when I was growing up. But around the same time that I became a prize runner and started to bring joy to other people, my relationship with my father started to become more challenging. I was a teenager and I started to have different needs.

My father wasn't a big communicator, but I always knew that he always had the best of intentions. I knew that running these kinds of races and winning made him proud. It gave me joy knowing that he was happy. He was a good man who loved his family and all he wanted to do was provide for us. Having been raised very poor in Mexico, just being here in America was a symbol of success for him. My father was the embodiment of the immigrant culture of the day.

Like most people around us, his view was: *Hey, we are lucky to be here! Just having a minimum paying job with benefits is success. That is all we strive for.*

He was famous for saying, "Que mas quieres?" *What else do you want?*

I heard these words coming from my father so often that I think they started to plant similarly limiting beliefs in my mind.

Why was I here?

Who am I?

Am I that boy with big dreams?

Should I even bother striving to make them come true?

Or am I here to go through the motions, go with the flow, and stay in my comfort zone?

I began to move away from my power and didn't even know it. Society and limiting beliefs were an outside influence that began to limit my potential.

The part of me that wanted to make my father proud took me out of my natural element of possibility. With my attention diverted in this way, I eventually became less joyous, and more focused on money. I was trying to be somebody that I wasn't. It took me out of my essence.

THE JOY OF PHYSICAL MOVEMENT

Physical movement is naturally connected to joy. If you can connect back to your natural essence of movement, this joy can be reignited. Reconnecting to your body will return you to a more natural way of moving your body. It's something that you already have, that you were born with, and it is possible for you to rediscover the joy that comes with physical movement.

Did Physical Movement Ignite My Joy, or Did Joy Ignite My Physical Movement?

When someone is joyous, they move their body with joy.

You can feel that, right?

When I am feeling good, when I am feeling joy, I can move my body more freely. There is less constriction in my movement.

Joy feeds physical movement—or does physical movement feed joy?

I remember the joy I felt when I was playing outside as a little boy. I would take off my shoes and start moving and running and it felt so good! Joy and physical movement work hand in hand; they feed each other. If you are not feeling good, then you can start to feel good by moving your body. It all comes back to the fact that the natural essence of moving ignites joy.

You can see that moving is joyful and that joy inspires movement. It is also clear that genuine joy can come from being really present in your life, by living fully in the process of what life brings to you. Being present can ignite joy and can be a bridge to moving your body with joy as well.

How I Lost the Natural Essence of Joy: Get Those Knees Up!

Somewhere in the timeline of our culture, running started to be used as a punishment. Although it sounds absurd, in elementary or middle school, we were actually punished with running.

How can physical movement be a punishment?

Somehow, a connection was built between punishment and moving our bodies. We became conditioned to feel this way. The result was that physical movement became equated with low mood, vibration, and frequency. Moving your body in that low frequency can only have a negative effect on your state of mind and body.

Because of the social conditioning of my culture, I started to lose that essence of joy by equating the moving of my body with punishment. In addition, I was reduced to moving my body in a very superficial way.

From coaches, athletes most often hear advice like:

- Get your knees up.
- Make your stride longer.
- Start quicker.
- Move faster.

This is a very superficial way of looking at moving our bodies. In our lives, we are given similarly superficial advice. We are told to move our lives forward faster. We are rushed off to school, and then rushed into a starting a career and family. We become superficial in our quests for success.

For me as a young man, this social conditioning started to affect how I moved my body. The superficial practice of moving my body forward became a fixed mentality. Soon, I wasn't connected to my body anymore. The more connected I was to my quest for success, the more I was taken out of my natural essence.

In other areas of my life, I tried to be successful according to the rules of my culture, my father, and my school. This superficial pursuit took me out of my natural essence as well. I can see now that they worked hand in hand. How I moved my body and how I lived my life progressively took me out of my natural essence. The end result was that I no longer felt good; the connection and joy of living was no longer present.

The superficial way of moving my body and living my life created the impression of a productive existence, but it was an illusion. I reached goals — points of success that I was told I should reach — but any sense of achievement was only temporary. The goals I met never brought me true fulfillment or happiness.

What are your goals?

If they are superficial in nature, they will never bring you fulfillment.

Some, for example, might think that success and fulfillment are going to come when they lose thirty pounds, or when they put ten million dollars in their bank account. For me during this time, I thought success was going to come if I ran this fast or when I could lift this amount of weight. There was never true fulfillment to be found in the reaching of these goals.

Neither could it be found in graduating from high school or going to college. It was all an illusion. The fulfillment that I needed remained elusive. My outer self could feel the illusion, and my inner self felt the lack of joy. There was a suffering and a void inside me.

Even when I had broken school records, national records, and qualified for the Olympics, I remained unfulfilled. My happiness was short lived until another goal was conquered, and so on, and so on.

I know now what was happening to me; it happens to young people all the time. We adults need to stop putting our only focus on *instructing* our youth and instead, preserve their natural joyous movement. As adults, we need to shift our mentality, put our foot down, reconnect, and help ourselves remember the joy.

How I Rediscovered My Essence of Joy

At the same time, I was suffering and feeling that void inside me, other challenging life experiences happened to me.

That's how I was thinking at the time: *All these bad things are happening to me.*

I always thought they were happening *to me*. But in reality, they were happening *for me*. They were giving me an opportunity to rediscover my joy, to bring me back to that natural essence. Life will be life — it has a magical but natural way of causing havoc for us, but it's only reflecting back to you what's already within your energy field.

It wasn't until I got injured that my whole life changed. I had qualified for the 1996 Olympics in Atlanta, and then, I tore my hamstring. I was two months away from achieving my life-long dream of going to the Olympics when I was brought down to the ground.

This was the worst thing that had ever happened to me. I was devastated.

I thought: *Why is this happening to me? Why, after all these years of training and hard work, have I been brought down to the ground?*

That moment of suffering, when I was literally dropped to the ground and stopped in my tracks — that was also the moment when I rediscovered my joy. At the time, of course, it didn't seem like it, but that was the beginning of rediscovering the inner joy that I once had physically, in my body, and in my life.

After that traumatic injury happened, my body and my spirit were torn. I lost connection to myself. I lost my identity. I was an emotional mess. I even lost the ability to dance. I knew that suffering was not my natural state. I knew there was more. I craved fulfillment.

During my recovery, I had some time to think about my racing career up to that point. When I looked back at my races, I remembered one race that I ran at the University of Southern California (USC) that felt completely different from all the other races.

I remembered thinking: *Wow, this feels really different.*

Even how I ran my race was different. At the same time, there was a vaguely familiar feeling to it. Later, I would identify that familiar feeling as the one I had when I ran around as a child, but I didn't know it at the time. It was the feeling of moving while being present in the moment.

During that first week after my traumatic injury, I spent some time watching recordings of my races. When I was watching that particular race, I kept rewinding the VHS tape to watch it again. I kept rewinding it, playing it, and rewinding it again, driving my family crazy.

I looked so different in that video. I looked joyously happy and I was moving so effortlessly. I could remember running past the finish line that day. I just kept running, like in the movie *Forrest Gump*, when they had to tell him to stop. I kept running until the end of the track. There was a gate there that stopped me — literally — from going outside of the track. I broke the California State University (Cal State) Long Beach school record that day. That was the race that gave me the opportunity to eventually represent Mexico in world-class competitions.

That race was in 1994. There had been many races since then.

I wondered: *What did I do? What did I do in this race that I didn't do after?*

Now, I understand why that race was so different. I was completely present in the moment. That race gave me a glimpse of what I used to be. I was so absorbed in the experience of every movement that I failed to see the finish line.

Isn't that how life should be lived?

To be able to be completely in the experience of the moment, not thinking about the past or worrying about future?

I work out on the track a lot, and there are a lot of kids out there training. It pains me to see how they are punished with running. Like I said before, running is just a movement. It should be a joy, but some of these kids are crying as they are running around the track — it kills me to see that. Bringing the joy back to movement is one of my strongest desires, especially for children like these.

We have been conditioned to define the road to success as:

- Hard work
- Pain
- Conquering goals

It doesn't have to be that way. Success is better defined as a joyous moment-to-moment experience that fuels true fulfillment.

Think about the baby who knows intuitively that the feeling of falling is just a part of moving forward. There is such natural joy in a baby's pursuits. I envision that whenever I see kids suffering with movement.

And if the baby falls when he takes that step, it doesn't feel like failure, does it?

When you picture the fallen baby, you can envision the caption: *I fell after taking that step, but hey, this is a part of me moving forward.*

THE JOY OF BEING IN THE MOMENT

Watching the way babies and children move enables you to see what it's like to be present within the journey. Babies don't look outside of themselves to feel like they are successful. They are only focused on taking that first step. There is such joy in that. When you are older, taking off your shoes and feeling the earth beneath your feet is a similar kind of joy.

You can maintain this natural ability, stay truly connected to your body, and keep this joyful essence. When goals are created using this essence, they are never superficial. Setting a goal from essence is key to achieving fulfillment even when you fail to reach your goals. When you lose the connection to your essence by being in your head, you can't achieve true fulfillment. When you set goals while being connected to your essence, you give yourself a better shot at not only reaching your goals, but at opening up to the possibility of achieving something higher. It is a win-win even if you fall short.

Whether your goal is to run the best business you can, be the best athlete you can, or become the best educator you could possibly be, if you are present and connected to your essence, you can gain happiness and true fulfillment.

Children have the natural ability to live in the present and to harness their potential. They don't even have to think about it. We need to learn from them. They remind us of what we can be. Children have no anxiety about the future and they easily forget the past. They are all about the moment. They don't think about the walk when they are trying to crawl.

Closing the Gap

Closing the gap refers to bringing yourself back to a balanced, happy state after something happens in your life. Children have a natural ability to close the gap. When they fall, they naturally get up. When they feel an emotion, they feel it completely; all that exists in that moment is that emotion. Then they bounce back. In fact, they are able to feel the opposite emotion in a matter of seconds.

Children have this innate ability to close the gap but most adults have lost that ability.

Why?

Here are a few reasons why closing the gap is so hard for us:

- We have been conditioned to keep the gaps open because of what we are told success is, or what we equate success to be.

- When we fall, we don't just get up and start again. We put energy into feeling bad about the fall, and this keeps the gap between failure and success open.

- We are often thinking like this: *I am not where I am supposed to be. I am not who I am supposed to be.* In doing so, we expand the gap between fulfillment and lack of fulfillment.

- When you identify yourself with an emotion or experience and won't let go, you are keeping that emotional gap open.

- Adults often need to see concrete evidence of their value to the outside world before they can feel worthy of happiness, so this gap is out of their control.

- Adults worry incessantly about the future and this makes it impossible to stay in the present.

If you are fretting constantly about your identity and value to the outside world, you can get so stuck in your head that you lose touch with your essence. If you are in this state, you must rediscover how to let go of your negative emotions by being present in the moment.

Movement can help you to do that. To be present within your movement can help you carry that mentality over to all the other parts of your life.

Be Circular, Not Linear

After I had my traumatic injury and I was watching my race at USC, I could see my body's net movement was forward, but what stood out to me was how much my body bounced. It was interesting for me to realize that I was watching a great deal of up-and-down movement in a race that resulted in my fastest time.

How can that be so?

Runners and other athletes are trained to move forward linearly, with as little wasted motion as possible. It was strange that so much bouncing resulted in such a fast time.

I studied my motion and that is when I made an interesting connection: I ran so fast *because* I was bouncing.

When you see kids move with joy, they bounce. Kids love to bounce. I was moving with joy that day and that's why the bouncing was evident. You must look closely at the play of forces in motion to understand what was happening during my race.

Here is what I discovered:

- Bouncing involves a circular movement in space.

- Initially, force is generated downward and then force is generated upward.

- The body coming up is the natural response to forces being applied down to the ground.

- The *upward* force at the end of the bounce becomes the *forward* force of the runner.

In other words, my movement forward was the result of bouncing up and down. And bouncing up and down was the result of applying power down while my body harnessed it. Since up and down is bouncing, then forward movement was the result of the bounce.

Finally, don't forget that the bounce is an expression of joy. I broke an NCAA Division I school record that day because of joy!

Bouncing relies on the power of downward movement. It is interesting that moving downward is always talked about negatively. Kids are always advised to rise up. There is no attention paid to forces being applied down; everything is about moving up. In life, there is a similar situation. We are always focusing on wanting to move up. There is no connection down to the ground. There is no connection to our planet.

After I made the connection about bounciness enhancing my race, I began to explore this idea and consider its applications. Moving forward physically with more efficiency and with more power, grace, and flexibility is about being circular. It is about being bouncy, having a balance between connecting down and moving up and forward. Our bodies are like a vessel whose power can be harnessed if you can find the right balance.

It was such an exciting time and I had many new questions to explore:

- How does this apply to different kinds of movement?

- How can this help track athletes to train?

- Can it help other athletes as well?

- Does this idea apply to other parts of life?

If moving faster as an athlete had so much to do with circular forces and grounding power, it makes sense that moving in life is also about being connected to yourself, being able to ground your power, and being able to harness this power to move forward.

It follows that, in life, you need to balance circular forces also. Being really present in the moment, within yourself, and your process equals moving forward fastest in life.

In my previous training, I was always focusing on trying to reach my goal. In doing so, I was limiting my potential because I was out of balance. When your focus is only on the output, harmony is impossible. I had become very linear. When I look back at how I moved my body during this linear time, I can see there was no bounce up and down.

It reminds me now of the flat line that appears on a heart monitor when we die. There was no life in my body. There was no life to my life. Everything was so linear. Everything I did was only focused on trying to reach a destination as fast as I could.

When I look at myself in that USC race, the bouncing is clearly visible. There was no flat line; there was life, joyfully springing up and down. When I think about the process of coming back to life, I picture the flat line on that monitor transforming into a bouncing line. There is life in that bouncy line. There is liveliness in it. This is the way I want to live my life. It is my goal to show other people that they can live this way as well.

Working With Children and Professional Athletes

I am a trainer now. I work with professional athletes and I have trained an Olympian to win a gold medal. More than 99 percent of the college and professional athletes who have come to me for help have made great improvements after training with The Hart Method. My techniques simply help them to remind their bodies, minds, and spirits how to move with freedom so they can optimize their performance.

I often get emails and calls from athletes who tell me what I shared with them is still helping them, even years later. Several have said that they still hear my voice reminding them what to do. I truly believe that they are really hearing their own voice, created by the essence of their own body.

Adults are actually my most difficult clients because they have been coached for so long to move their body in a linear, superficial way. Children are my easiest clients. They don't have all the layers of beliefs that adults have accumulated — coming from coaches, TV, athletes, or parents — that I have to peel away.

My goal for all my clients, besides maximizing their on-the-field performance, is to apply the maxims of The Hart Method to their lives.

If I can help a child preserve their natural essence and expand from that, the possibilities are endless, not only for their performance, but for their whole lives. If I can help adults to shed their layers of false beliefs to get back to this natural essence, they will be able to see their potential again. Watching a person light up with joy when they make connections brings me joy and fulfillment. In that moment, I feel like I was able to change that person's life simply by helping them remember who they are.

One of my clients was a professional baseball player who once said to me, "If I had known this way of training when I started my career, I would have been a different baseball player."

I thought about it and agreed, but that view is shortsighted. My goal is not only to consider what athletes can achieve on the field, but also to consider what they can carry into the rest of their lives.

CHAPTER TWO

What Goes Down
Must Come Up

GROUNDING YOUR POWER

We take gravity for granted because we live within its force. You know that any object will drop to the ground without any effort on your part; you don't have to think about it.

What goes up must come down. This idea is ingrained in our psyche.

Picture the bouncing of a ball or the bouncing of a moving athlete. When you're visualizing the motion, it is natural to focus more on the bounce *up* than on the downward part of the motion. In any endeavor, people always appreciate the going up, but we rarely appreciate the coming down. We have become obsessed with results. We hardly ever marvel at the way someone throws a ball down, or admire the path of an athlete's foot towards the ground.

What part of an athlete's movement do we usually admire?

It is the upward or forward movement that catches our attention. However, it is actually the downward force that is responsible for the upward and forward motion. The power of motion comes from going down.

What goes *down* must come *up*. Understanding this idea can make all the difference—for your athletic endeavors, but also for your life.

I've told you about the traumatic injury that put a halt to my dream of becoming an Olympian. But that turned out to be a great opportunity for me. The Hart Method was born through that experience; it arose from the experience of falling down.

We tend to think of falling down as a failure from which we need to recover. Although it doesn't feel good, falling down can be the best thing that can happen to you. In actuality, I have found that moving forward in life can't happen *without* falling down. However, life doesn't have to strike you down dramatically the way it struck me in order for you to begin.

Think about your own life and try to remember a time when you fell down, either physically, emotionally, or spiritually.

On that day, imagine if you had taken this attitude: *I know that whatever comes down must come up. Moving forward in life can't happen without falling down.*

This kind of perspective can make such a difference. You will have times when you will fall down; this is a natural part of life. With the right attitude, however, new possibilities can arise from falling down. When you take this concept to heart, it is the first step to living your ideal life.

Putting My Foot Down

Your life can change in a moment. For an athlete, who depends on the optimal working of the body, a single injury can be life-changing.

Your body is like a team with many players, and can only work optimally when the players are in harmony. The leader of a successful team is not driven by his ego and is humble enough to admit his faults without pointing fingers. The leader has the ability to make everyone better. Your body craves the same connection and leadership. When your body parts are not working in harmony, your body tends to break down.

This is what happened to me. After my injury in 1996, I was reduced to my lowest state. I needed answers.

I wondered: *How did I end up here?*

Looking for help, I got in my 1965 red Mustang in the middle of winter and drove to Houston, Texas, to train under Tom Tellez, who also coached my idol, Carl Lewis.

I was soon training alongside my childhood hero. I had admired and looked up to Carl Lewis my whole life, and this should have been the realization of a dream. But my most vivid memory of training with him is when he came up to me at practice, pinched my side roll, and told me to lay off the burritos.

I was in a dark place. I had gone from fearlessly moving forward despite any obstacles to living in fear of making mistakes. The trauma of my injury left me afraid of moving forward with my body and afraid of moving forward in life. I had a great deal to learn about myself.

Coach Tom Tellez gave me a key to the process on the very first day he worked with me.

After watching me run, he told me, "Put your foot down."

I had no idea what he meant. To help me understand, he pointed out a little kid running on the track.

He said, "Look. *That's* how you should run. That's how everybody should run."

I watched the kid running.

As I watched his little feet hit the track, I thought: *Put your foot down*.

That moment was an awakening for me, an enlightening point in my life.

I thought: *Carl Lewis, who has won nine Olympic gold medals, and his coach, who is considered one of the best in the history of track and field, are simply telling me to put my foot down. This must be the key to winning. Put your foot down. Yes!*

How simple it all became. This single concept opened the door to recovery for me, recovery for my body, recovery as an athlete, and recovery for other areas of my life, as you will see.

Keeping Your Focus in the Moment

What did Coach Tellez mean when he said, "Put your foot down."?

What did I see when I was watching the kid run around the track?

Why was it a key to my recovery?

To answer these questions, let's go back to what we know about children. As we've discussed before, children move naturally, with joy and abandon. They are connected to their natural essence — the inner self they were born with. In the process of becoming adults, we lose that connection and must work to get it back and keep it. Our natural essence is the source of our power.

The bare essence of movement is visible when you watch children move their bodies. When children walk or run, they put each foot down, one after another, to move forward. They move their stride forward gracefully.

We lose this natural way of being as we get older; our focus shifts away from putting the foot down. We get caught up in expectations and make attempts to force our goals into reality. To get your power back in life, you also must put each foot down and keep your focus there.

There are many ways in which your focus can shift as time goes on.

Here are some of them:

- For some, it shifts ahead in time — you worry about the future.

- For others, it shifts behind in time — you obsess about the past.

- You may be worrying about your performance, or thinking about an injury.

- You may shift your attention to extraneous details around you — like wondering what your competition is doing.

- You may get caught up in the expectations of others.

- You may focus exclusively on your goals, attempting to force them into reality.

When your focus shifts away from that childlike way of putting your foot down, you begin to move your body without awareness. This causes a separation between your body and mind. You become obsessed about reaching goals without being present in the experience of the journey. This obsession often leads to having anxiety about the future.

To get access to your power in life, you must return to the childlike way of putting your foot down, and you must regain your focus. In other words, you must return to your natural essence. In my athletic work after the injury, once I decided to put my foot down physically, I moved with more ease and my body started to feel a lot better.

During my road to recovery, I searched for answers everywhere. I became absorbed in reading about movement and kinesiology, hoping to learn more about moving with efficiency. I also read self-development books. I was struck by how many of these books spoke about reconnecting to yourself to harness your power. This process wasn't about developing new strength; it was about remembering how to access the power you already possessed. I started to understand that the advice Coach Tellez had given me could also apply to the rest of my life. I needed to put my foot down in my life.

Even before my injury, I had life issues that needed addressing, including relationships that were out of harmony. It came to me that, in all areas of my life, I had to put my foot down to rediscover who I truly was. When I began to understand the concept of putting my foot down in my training, I could transfer the process from my body to the rest of my life.

Recovery from my injury was difficult at the beginning, but, eventually, I started to rise up. To make a personal connection between my body and my life, I had to be receptive to it—I had to have an open heart. That is when real change started to occur for me. I started to feel my power, and this was only the beginning. When I began to tap into that power, I started to move my life with more ease and everything in my world started to fall into place.

Don't forget—for any of this to happen, I had to fall down. This truth fits right in with what we learned in the last section: *moving forward can't happen until you fall down.*

Power Versus Fear

This idea of putting your foot down is the first principle of The Hart Method, called *the ground maxim*. Although the concept is simple, I don't want to mislead you into thinking these changes were easy. Putting your foot down is easier said than done!

A fear-based mentality is hard to overcome. For athletes, fear causes distinct changes in their course of motion. These changes can cause catastrophic problems for an athlete. For example, it can affect a pitcher's windup and delivery, wreck a golf swing, a skater's jump, or a basketball player's shot from the foul line. To analyze the problem, you need to break down the elements of the motion.

I will use the running motion as an example because it is a necessary skill for many athletes. You all know what running looks like, but if we break it down here, you will understand how fear may impact the motion.

You already know that running consists of alternating the two legs to push the body forward. For most of the motion, one leg is ahead of your torso — *the lead leg* — and the other behind — *the trail leg*.

Imagine yourself running. Let's describe the motion starting with the right leg leading:

1. You hit the ground beneath you with the right foot and push forward.

2. Your right foot bounces off the ground and the right leg becomes the trail leg behind you as your body moves ahead.

3. At the same time, the left leg lifts and comes forward to become the lead leg.

4. You hit the ground with the left foot, push forward off the left foot, and the left leg becomes the trail leg behind you.

Now, consider this question: If you are trying to run very fast and you are afraid of failure, what part of the motion will you think about the most?

Here is what I have found: I have learned that the runner who is thinking fearfully will focus on the trail leg the entire time he is running.

Why?

It is because the trail leg is *behind*. The fearful runner desperately wants to get it to the front as fast as possible.

Thinking about the trail leg is fear-based thinking; you are worried about getting that leg from back to front.

For years, this is exactly the way I was running. I have found that this fear-based focus is very common for athletes. We are all so programmed to move forward, ever forward. Whatever is trailing behind we are compelled to drag forward as quickly as possible. This is an unnatural way of moving.

Remember the child that my coach pointed out to me on the track?

You can look at a child to refresh your mind and remind yourself what a natural stride looks like. Children don't worry about the trailing leg. When they run — like when they first began to walk — they stride forward moving one leg, and the trailing leg naturally follows the movement of their body.

The natural essence of movement is to *focus on the leg that is right beneath you*. This is how to access your natural power.

If you are an athlete moving with a fear-based mentality, you aren't accessing your natural power and you will never realize your potential.

Where does the fear-based mentality come from?

I believe that it was programmed into your being by your surroundings — by family, coaches, and society. It may not be intentional, but these forces condition you to lose the natural freedom of movement that connects with your essence.

I can give you an example from my own life. As a child, I played soccer for years. My father didn't come to my games very often, but I had a mentor who would pick me up and take me to the games.

I remember one day, he was dropping me off at home after a soccer tournament. I always dreaded the moment I got dropped off. On the weekends, my father was always out there in the yard with his brothers and friends, barbecuing. When I got out of the car, carrying my water jug and looking bedraggled after playing multiple games, I had to pass right by them on my way to the house. Every time, my father and my uncles would pepper me with questions and comments.

"Did you win?"

"No." Unfortunately, that was almost always true.

"Ugh, you suck."

They always made a comment like that. Of course, that didn't feel good to me.

One day I said to myself: *The next time I am going to lie and tell them that I did win.*

The next time I got out of the car, as usual, they asked me, "Did you win?"

I lied and said, "Yes, we did."

"Did you score?"

My heart sank. I wasn't prepared for that.

"No."

"Ugh, you suck."

Okay, I thought: *Next time I will lie about scoring goals.*

After the next game:

"Did you win?"

"Yes."

"Did you score?"

"Yes."

"How many goals?"

"One."

"Ugh, that's it?"

I took it further and lied about scoring more goals. I told them I scored four goals and they said, "Wow, the other team must have been playing without a goalie."

That was the mentality. That was the culture I was brought up in. No matter what I did, I wasn't good enough. I took that into how I lived my life. No matter what I did, it wasn't good enough.

In my experience, most adults have a similar feeling inside. You and I may not have had exactly the same experiences in our lives, but in some way, it is likely you have been programmed to feel that whatever you are is not good enough. As we discussed in the last chapter, social conditioning has a way of disconnecting you from your essence. It may be a direct result of the way our society pushes us to move faster—and forward, always forward.

Focusing on the trailing foot can be a difficult habit to break. You must consciously choose to change. Talk to yourself if it helps.

I started by saying the words in my head as I ran: *Just put your foot down. Just put your foot down.*

Once I started to succeed in putting that foot down— the foot that was right beneath me—I discovered that there was no longer any need to worry about that back leg. The trail leg naturally came forward. Over time,

I came to understand that when yo
down, your body is in a position to ap
force because you are right on top of you
gravity. With a shift slightly forward, you can
more power than ever.

By putting your foot down, you can connect with your
natural power, and move with joy and freedom.

Staying in the Moment

Over time, I noticed something else interesting. The
practice of putting my foot down kept my attention in
the moment — in the right here and right now. This is
no coincidence; staying in the moment is required to
access your power and you can't put your foot down
without it.

Imagine if, instead of staying in the moment, you are
focused on the past. In this case, you have a fear-based
mentality. When you have this kind of focus, you are
bringing your past to the future.

To understand this, try the exercise below:

- Visualize your body moving with a focus on the
  trailing leg.

- Imagine yourself running and watch that trailing
  leg in slow motion.

ve the leg forward and

is effectively bringing
eg — into the future — the

v, you are either thinking
and this is a fear-based
n thinking about what is
happening right here and right now.

Now, visualize your body moving again, but think about your leg dropping toward the ground instead. That is a power position right there. It's not easy to do.

Why is it so difficult?

It's difficult because you and I are programmed to live in our past or in our future. In addition, we are programmed to live in our minds and egos. We are constantly comparing ourselves to others, trying to move faster than the competition, trying to get ahead and stay ahead of everyone else. Acting from this position distracts your attention from the moment and in doing so, keeps you from connecting to your power.

You limit your potential when you try to move your body with this kind of mentality. Sometimes, I think that the opposite may also be true — that moving in this fear-based way can impact your mind and the way you live your life, leading you to manage your life in a fear-based way as well.

Which came first—the chicken or the egg? The fear of losing ground in life, or the fear of losing a race?

Either way, one will affect the other because it's the mentality that is out of balance.

We may not be able to find the answer to this question, but in either case, you must pay attention to your mentality, both for your physical performance and for your life.

Getting Results: The Seen and Unseen

You want to achieve results from your efforts. We all do. It is likely that you admire people who have won awards and other achievements. You probably want to achieve such goals yourself and there is nothing wrong with that. Unfortunately, most of us have been programmed to work on achieving results without doing the inner work that is necessary for authentic success.

If you focus on winning awards, your attention is not in the moment. It is on the future.

Furthermore, if your attention is on the awards you want to win, your motivation is not internal at all; it is completely external. With such a results-based mentality, you will be unable to concentrate on the leg beneath you. You will be unable to *put your foot down* in the way we have discussed.

Although it may be difficult, changing your mental focus away from striving for rewards is necessary.

Here are some suggestions to keep in mind as you work on this:

- Move your body and focus on the leg that is dropping down. This will help you with the inner work because it is the same kind of process.

- Concentrate on staying in the moment.

- You must work hard to address the false beliefs you have, especially the ones that are self-limiting.

- Internal work is not easy. Some of this is ugly, dark work and you won't want to do it. Don't give up.

- Be truthful and be authentic, no matter how hard it is.

- Do the inner work and trust that you will accomplish more than you can imagine.

- If you have been fixated on results for a long time, your mind will habitually create superficial goals to strive for, whether they are authentic or not. You can stop doing this if you try.

- Be authentic even if you sacrifice the external pat on the back. Acknowledge your own progress and celebrate all successes, no matter how small. Let yourself feel good.

If you can succeed in moving your body in a way that connects to your essence, you will trigger the sending of a message to the universe that will change your life. It will enable you to *magnetize* what you need to move your life forward in the most fulfilling way.

All these important changes are internal and unseen. Working on the unseen, in the dark, is one of the hardest parts of this process. Because it is not visible, other people won't appreciate it at all. It is natural to look for approval and appreciation—even applause. It helps you to feel good about yourself. Doing unseen work will give you none of that.

Still, in all things, what you give is what you get. The power you apply—in the moment and down toward the ground — is what results in the opposite leg coming up. What you give to yourself is what you get in return.

We've been discussing the nuts and bolts of the process of change, but don't forget the joy. Always remember that it is the down action that creates the bounce—and the bounce equals joy. Joy is and always should be at the root of your physical movement and a part of all your life quests.

Moving your body in this new way will clear the layers that get in the way of communication between body, mind, and heart. The body talks and it's up to you to listen. The body — in its whole form that includes mind and heart — will show you the way.

THE POWER OF FAILURE

It is likely that you see failure as a negative thing. Society teaches you to try to avoid failure at all costs. You may hold yourself back from moving forward because you are afraid to fail. However, you may not be aware that within failure is great power.

When you move your body forward, with one leg coming down toward the ground and your body leaning at a 5 percent angle, you are, in effect, falling. We associate falling with failing. But, in order for the body to move forward with momentum, it has to fall forward. You must experience the feeling of falling in order to move forward.

You need to make mistakes, you need to fall down, and you need to fail in order to move forward in life. The key is learning to fail with awareness. The key is learning to fail while trusting that failure is a necessary part of moving forward.

This is the *gravity maxim* of The Hart Method: *Forward movement is not possible without falling.* If you're not falling, your forward movement is only an illusion.

You Will Have Support

After I had my traumatic injury in 1996 and I was laying there on the ground knowing my dreams had probably come to an end, I remember being very conscious of the contact between my body and the ground. Oddly, I felt tremendous support from the ground. There was this intense feeling of failure, and all my dreams came crashing down, but the ground was there to support me. Nobody else was around at that moment — no family or girlfriend — but I felt this tremendous support from the ground.

We need the ground. We need the ground in order to generate and harness power to move forward.

In life, the ground is a metaphor for the support that is all around you. You are always going to have that. You will have support, both for your body and for your spirit. If you fall down physically, you will be supported by the world around you. You will always have the ground, and when you fall down in other ways, you will also be supported, no matter what.

This experience was the beginning of my awareness of the connection between my body, my life, and my environment. Connecting with this natural way of being was magical for me.

After Coach Tellez pointed out the child running on the track and told me that was how everyone should run, I began to change my perspective. Soon, I realized that, not only should we should run that way, but that is also how we should live our lives. We need to return to our natural essence.

I started to understand that there was a way we could get our essence back. A lot of the kids I work with are my easiest clients because they are already in connection with their essence. They just need to continue and expand. My older clients are my hardest clients, because they must shed many false layers before they can get to their essence once again. Most of my work on myself has been given to shedding these layers to get me back in connection with the natural essence I had as a child.

When it starts to happen for you, it will feel magical.

I remember feeling: *Wow, this is amazing.*

My body felt like a reflection of the universe and to feel this connection was magical.

Trust the Process

Trusting the process of change is vital. Learning to see your movements and your life from a different perspective is difficult. If you don't trust the process, you will give up too easily. As we've already talked about, if you get caught up in achieving results, you will force your life to go in particular directions just for the sake of those results. You will be acting out of fear and any achievements will be unfulfilling.

Many of us, including many athletes, get into this fear-based mentality of trying to catch up or move forward because we fear falling behind. Trust the leg that is coming down and stay in that moment. Trust whatever is happening in your life, even if it looks like it's not getting you close to your dreams or goals. Trust that your actions are going to create the results you need. In fact, you are likely to surpass your expectations.

Put your focus in the moment—right here and right now. Trust that, and know that it is going to move you in the direction that is going to bring true joy and true fulfillment.

Acknowledge Results

When you begin to successfully focus in the present moment, don't forget to acknowledge the results that come from your efforts:

- Start simply. Acknowledge the dropping of the leg down toward the ground. Celebrate when you succeed in focusing completely on putting your foot down.

- As the opposite leg is coming up, you need to acknowledge that also, because that only happened because you put your foot down. Acknowledge the knee of that leg coming up and forward.

- It isn't about your body alone. When you see results of doing your inner work, you need to celebrate those moments too.

- When you are doing the unpleasant and difficult work that only you can see, congratulate yourself.

- When you persist in staying focused on the moment, take note of your success.

- Pay attention to how you feel: *Wow, look at that. My leg is coming forward, and I'm not even trying to do that. It feels so good.*

When your body is moving forward with full intensity, you may not be able to take the time to acknowledge each element, but during drills and slower movements, you can be conscious and appreciative.

Acknowledge those results and celebrate them with joy. When you acknowledge the results of your physical efforts, when you feel that leg coming forward effortlessly, you will build momentum. And it will feel good.

You may feel like your body is bouncing more. Don't force the bounce; let it happen naturally, as children do. As you practice putting your foot down, as you notice changes and acknowledge the results you are getting, you will create this bouncing. The ground will be there as a platform for you to bounce your body up and forward. It will ignite joy. It feels good and will create momentum.

In life, it is the same thing. While you are working on your false beliefs and the unseen dark spots of yourself and you feel like you are moving forward effortlessly, celebrate your results with joy. Everything will start to click. Acknowledge your progress, be present, and trust your process as you gain momentum. Don't forget that it is your internal work — working on the stuff you didn't want to do — that has gotten you this far.

Have you ever seen the *Under Armor* commercial starring Michael Phelps?

It shows him training three times a day, in all seasons, even in the freezing cold.

The tagline of the commercial is: *What you do in the dark is what puts you in the light.*

I think that is the perfect metaphor for the unseen work you are doing. It's true. What we do in the dark is what puts us in the light. Celebrate your progress.

TRUST AND EXPAND FORWARD

When you step forward and drop your leg down toward the ground, you need to trust that the ground will be there and that it will support you. This trust is the foundation of expanding forward.

As we've discussed, the ground functions as the platform for your body to move forward and up. In your life, the same kind of trust is required for expansion. No matter what difficulties you are going through, trust that whatever you need will be provided for you. You need to know that the ground will support you before you can move forward.

Take the First Step

Imagine me running, but not leaning forward. I am raising my legs up and down, really fast, but I'm not going anywhere. This is what would happen if I was afraid to fall. To run, your body must lean forward.

But if you lean forward, you might fall. You must risk falling — failing — in order to go anywhere physically.

Remember: *Moving forward in life can only happen by falling down.*

You must risk falling in order to move forward in life. You need to take that first step. You need to open up your heart to opportunities and experiences that will only come when you risk falling.

I have been that person who was too afraid to step forward. Before my accident, I was moving my body as fast as I could, which gave me the illusion of moving fast, but I wasn't taking that step forward because I was afraid to fail.

In life, I was acting in that same way. From the outside, it looked like I was moving beautifully through life, but I really wasn't, because I was afraid to make mistakes. I was afraid to fail. If I did so in private, I was afraid to share that I failed. It was all an illusion. It was a lie.

Once I discovered in my physical training that in order for my body to move forward, it needs to feel the sensation of falling, I decided to use the same strategy in other areas of my life. When I took risks, it did feel like I was falling, but it wasn't until I let myself feel that way that I started to move forward. I made mistakes and learned that I didn't need to be afraid to share my failures. Now, I look forward to failures and falling because I know it's a sign of moving forward. It all started from that first step.

To begin, you need to take that first step forward.

I have been around a lot of people who remind me of how I used to be. They are afraid to fail. They are afraid to make mistakes. On the outside, it may seem like these people have perfect lives, but I remember what that was like.

Think about this whenever you ever look at someone and think: *That person has a great life, and I don't. I need to make changes so I can be like them.*

What you see may well be an illusion. When you compare your life with another person's life, you may make superficial changes that create your own illusion of success. It becomes a vicious cycle. Instead, take the risk and step forward. Go deep within yourself and work on the inner you.

Your only job is to get back the joy of movement, go back to your essence, and open your heart to the experience of life. Make mistakes, experience failure, and develop an authentic big vision of where you want your life to go.

We will talk more about developing your big vision later in this book. The big vision is the driving force that you will need to direct your forward movement.

Failure Is Success in Progress

I once saw this quote on a T-shirt: *Failure is success in progress.*

Isn't that just what we need to believe?

We are so conditioned to think that failing is a bad thing. It's time for us to adapt and incorporate this new mentality.

It is almost like learning a new dance:

- Drop your leg down.
- Put your foot down.
- Work on the unseen.
- Get back your power.
- Acknowledge the results.

This dance can create a true art form that depicts who we really are, not only as individuals, but also as a collective. Failure is success in progress, and success, to me, is true fulfillment of potential.

You can apply this mentality—this dance—to every level of our society.

There are so many ways it could be applied. Healthcare, for instance, could use an overhaul. Our medical establishments often resort to superficial ways of healing the body and many times, the treatments create other problems. We need true healing solutions instead. Education is another area that needs revision. Our public education system has a results-based mentality that doesn't serve our children as well as another method could.

The simple action of putting your foot down could lead to making real change, not just in how you move your body and in your individual life, but in the world.

Momentum

One of the races Carl Lewis ran many times was the hundred-meter sprint. This race is over in a flash — an Olympian will run it in under ten seconds. Carl was notorious for starting behind everybody else. Several coaches who knew I trained with Carl told me that he would probably run a couple of tenths of a second faster if he got out of the starting blocks more quickly. But they didn't understand that he had his blocks set up in a certain way to maximize his acceleration later in the race.

Maximizing his acceleration also resulted in minimizing his slowing down phase, which is the time, later in the race, when most runners lose speed. It always appeared that Carl was moving faster and faster during the course of the race. But it wasn't that he was getting faster; it was that he was maximizing his acceleration. There was a point in the race at which everybody else in the race was losing their speed, but not Carl.

I believe that Carl was a master of momentum despite being last out of the blocks. He carried over this philosophy onto his yearly training cycle, and his entire career.

Understanding this about Carl helped me develop another element of my training method. It is certainly an advantage to maximize your acceleration, both in your athletic training and in your life. To do this, you should consider what encourages and inhibits momentum.

These are some actions that may inhibit momentum:

- Focusing on achieving results quickly
- Lack of awareness
- Not staying in the moment
- Setting superficial goals
- Not doing inner work along with outer work
- Being stuck in a belief system that puts you down and says you're not good enough

Physically, if you get caught up in achieving results right at the beginning of starting a new venture, you are likely to decelerate quickly. In other words, you will start to burn out. You can visualize how this would be true in running races and in other athletic endeavors. It is also true of business, education, and in careers of all kinds.

Someone who is trying to get in shape might start off really gung-ho about losing pounds and working out. You already know what happens to most people who start this way. They focus completely on superficial results, get disappointed, then decelerate, and before long, completely give up. They never have a chance to build up momentum.

Instead, you need to plan your movements in a way that keeps your momentum up, just like Carl did. Think big, but start small. Authentic results will come as you become aware of your body, as you get back the essence of moving your body in the moment. This can only come from gaining true awareness and not just being focused on results.

You are here for the long run. It's great to lose thirty or forty pounds and to reduce your body fat. It feels good, but it is also only temporary. It is the same for the other parts of your life. If your goals are superficial, you may achieve results, but they will be short-lived, and you will not be happy or fulfilled.

CHAPTER THREE

Integrity, Joy, Harmony, and Freedom

COMING BACK TO WHERE YOU ARE

Do you know what it is to be in integrity with yourself?

The word *integrity* is usually defined as *honesty*, or *keeping your word*, but that's not exactly what I mean here.

To be in integrity with yourself means:

- Being present with your body
- Having awareness
- Staying in the moment
- Being whole and complete
- Honoring your body
- Connecting to the ground

Being in integrity with yourself is what leads to harmony. If you honor your body, if you are in the present with your body, and are aware of your body, these things will lead you to this sense of integrity.

Integrity means to be whole and complete, to be present in the moment. This is the meaning of the *integrity maxim* of The Hart Method.

If your mind is elsewhere — in a way that is not aware and honoring your body, for instance — you are out of integrity.

Here are examples of thoughts that show you are not in integrity with yourself:

- Thinking badly about yourself: *I don't want this body. I don't like this body.*

- Constantly wishing you were different: *If only I weighed twenty-five pounds less, or had less body fat, then my body would be okay.*

- Always competing with others in your own mind: *I'll be happy when I'm as fast as him.*

- Comparing yourself to other people while you're working out: *No matter how much I exercise, I'll never have a figure as nice as hers.*

- Letting your mind wander while you are moving your body, instead of being in the moment.

The last item is something you might not notice. Your mind will easily go elsewhere when you are moving and exercising. You may have to work at keeping it from wandering.

When you are in integrity with yourself, you will feel focused, free, and joyful. You are connecting to your essence, and that will feel good. This is the *joy maxim* of The Hart Method.

Pay attention to your feelings. Feel the joy and celebrate your achievements. The more you celebrate, the more you will be in a joyful frame of mind, and the more you will manifest. Don't ignore your achievements. Allow yourself to feel joyful, to experience fully the gifts you have received. It feels good to give when the receiving is appreciated. We want to give more. That's how the universe works. It wants to give you more when you joyfully acknowledge its gifts.

Anything you do physically — dance, aerobics, skating, swimming, running, playing — is an opportunity to honor your body and be in integrity with your body. Come back to yourself. Being in integrity is what leads to being in joy.

Coming back to where you are is another way of describing a state of integrity. Coming back to the present moment, even if it is an experience you are not really enjoying, is part of the work you must do to be in joy.

Keep assessing the integrity of your body and your mind. This is the beginning of coming back to yourself.

Ask yourself questions like these:

Am I putting my foot down?

Am I connecting with the ground?

Am I in the moment with my body?

Am I in the moment with my mind?

Am I thinking about shopping during my power walk?

Am I focused on personal problems while I'm practicing with my team?

Coming back to yourself is the beginning of developing a powerful relationship with your body. As you flow into this power, you will feel the joy. You will feel the bounce that we talked about before.

At this point, take the opportunity to honor your body, one part at a time:

- Listen to your body. Use your senses to assess your inner self.
- Is your core engaged? Honor it.
- Honor your arms and legs that are moving for you.
- Are your shoulders loose? Honor them.
- Honor your organs that are working to sustain you.

- Communicate with your bones and ligaments.
- Honor your connection to yourself.

This process creates harmony and integrity. You are connecting back to yourself, back to the moment, and back to your potential. In connecting back to yourself, you will create something remarkable — a space of *nothingness*. The creative power of this space is astounding. It is in that space of nothingness where ideas arise. I have had my most creative inspirations after reconnecting with my body during physical exercise, whether it is walking or jogging.

We get so caught up in thinking about yesterday or tomorrow that we lose sight of the power that lies in the present moment. It exists in this space of nothingness. By engaging with your body, you can bring this awareness back to yourself and harness that power once again.

HARMONY IN PHYSICAL MOVEMENT IS A BRIDGE TO HARMONY IN LIFE

As a collective, we all desire to be in harmony with each other, especially during these times of racial tension and political unrest. We have become disconnected as a population, and, as individuals, we lack harmony between body and mind.

How can we expect to live in harmony with others when we lack harmony within ourselves?

The first step is really being in harmony with ourselves. This is the *harmony maxim* of The Hart Method. Start with your body; it has the potential to bring powerful change.

That is why I am deeply committed to my work with body dynamics. Everything starts with taking that first step. The aim of that first step is to find the harmony within your own body and that is the beginning of being in harmony with everything. When your physical parts are working in perfect harmony, they will become greater than the whole. And when we are all whole and in harmony, humanity can also become greater than the whole.

Honor Your Body

If you want to find harmony, you need to look inside yourself and create harmony within. In time, the process will extend beyond you, but you must begin within. Your body is the vehicle to bring out the awareness that is required.

To begin, honor your body. Whether you are thin or fifty pounds overweight, you must find a way to honor yourself. Your body is your own individual expression, your own unique and precious vessel. The first step is honoring yourself—loving yourself. Honor your organs, your bones, your ligaments, your tendons, and beyond. Honor your unique self for whoever you are. From there, you can progress to creating a sense of harmony through movement.

Coming Full Circle

To truly be in a harmonious state, you must have harmony in body as well as spirit; you must create a life of harmony. Everything is connected.

When you are making any kind of movement, your body automatically directs a complex set of coordinating actions. You are not conscious of these activities; they are involuntary. For example, when your arm is moved through a certain range in motion, the opposite leg automatically balances the movement. The right arm and the left leg move in harmony and are affected by each other. If you cut the movement short for the right arm or if you do damage to the right arm, the left leg will be affected.

There are hundreds of other examples of compensating and coordinating body movements. They are part of your natural physiology. This means that your body parts and motions are all interconnected and dependent on each other.

If the left leg is being affected by the right arm's movement, there will be another body part that will be affected by the left leg's movement. And so on and so on until it comes back to that right arm again.

If there is a body part that is being impacted by something you are doing, there will be an effect on other parts of the body. If one body part is damaged, it will affect the activity of other body parts.

If you are having a problem with one particular movement, it may have come about because of another issue. Being aware of the interconnected nature of your body can help you to identify the origin of problems you are having.

When you are analyzing your body movements, here are some questions for you to ask yourself:

- *Am I changing the angle of my motion in some way?*
- *Am I allowing the full range of motion?*
- *Am I moving with fear and cutting my movement short?*
- *Am I listening to what my body communicates?*

If you don't listen to your body, there will be consequences.

If you have sustained damage to a body part, your body may be saying: *Hey, look at me. Get some rest today!*

All body issues will always come back to how well you are paying attention to your body. Injuries and setbacks will be the result of not listening. If you are prone to injury, it is likely that you need to improve the way you communicate with your body.

Listening is a necessary part of honoring your body. It is needed to create *inner* harmony, and it is no surprise that it is also a necessary part of creating *outer* harmony. To maintain a healthy body, you need to listen. Likewise, to maintain healthy relationships, you also need to listen.

Sometimes, a coach comes to me for help because they know their team is out of harmony. There may be ego issues, arguments, or fights. When I work with teams, the importance of listening is one of the highlights of my counsel.

In these cases, my aim is to help the teammates see that when one person is negatively impacted by a situation, it affects the entire team. If you cause one person distress, it will spread all the way around, full-circle, and come back to you. If you're doing damage to another teammate, then you are doing damage to yourself.

Whenever I talk like this with a team, I see eyes opening. Many times, athletes lose sight of their impact on each other. When I help them understand, amazing changes can happen. When teammates truly listen to one another, a team works in perfect harmony without the presence of ego. The team becomes *one* and the whole becomes greater than the sum of all its parts.

When you listen and take care of yourself, your body and mind can maintain a full circle of health. If you listen and take care of the people around you, you will foster a healthy team.

If you ignore the needs of your body and mind, your aches, pains, injuries, and unhappiness will spread, full-circle. When you intentionally do damage to another person, it comes around, full-circle, and you will do damage to the team, and to yourself as well.

We are all connected here. We are all a different and essential part of this whole collective that we call humanity.

Building a Bridge to Others

Once you improve your body awareness and are in harmony with your body, you can begin to move your body in harmony. As we've already discussed, putting your foot down is the first step to creating a deep and powerful relationship with your body. When you understand this, you will truly be able to build bridges and connect with others in a powerful way.

I have witnessed this kind of transformation in my work with teams. First, the athletes need to understand the importance of being in harmony with their own bodies and movements. Then, I can help them carry over that philosophy in talking about the importance of being in harmony with the team.

When this works, coaches can see the difference. The team develops a different dynamic, one that is more about harmony and teamwork.

In some cases, the problem with a team may have been created by two players who don't like each other. Their lack of harmony can affect the whole team during practice and games. When I can get those players to understand how each person can impact the whole team positively or negatively, what a difference that can make!

When each individual understands how powerful they are, they will often elect to act in a more harmonious way. Showing the individual players the power of being in harmony helps them to make the connection between themselves. It feels really good. It is just like moving your body in a harmonious way. It feels good.

When a person feels this harmony, there is a sense of belief that comes with it. If they feel it within themselves, then it's easier to carry it over and treat others with that same type of awareness, which really makes a difference for a team — or for any relationship. In other words, when you feel true and egoless change within yourself, you want others to feel the same.

Do a Body Check

When you are doing physical exercise or simply walking, doing a body check is something that you can use to bring the awareness and focus back to yourself. The body check is a reflection of the first five maxims of the Hart Method: Ground, Gravity, Integrity, Joy, and Harmony.

1. The Ground Maxim: Put your foot down.
2. The Gravity Maxim: Be aware that forward motion can only be accomplished by falling down.
3. The Integrity Maxim: Be whole and complete, in the moment.
4. The Joy Maxim: Feel the joy that comes from connecting to your essence.
5. The Harmony Maxim: Honor the interconnected nature of your body and your world.

When you do a body check, notice if you are putting your foot down and can feel the connection between yourself and the ground. See that you are moving with the awareness that you must fall a little in order to move forward and that you are moving without fear.

Be sure you are moving your body in the moment, without allowing your mind to wander. Take time to feel the joy. Acknowledge, feel and honor your body — from bones and ligaments to organs and cells. Go within while you are moving your body, so it is like a meditative experience in motion.

Go through each of the maxims and give yourself the opportunity to come back to yourself.

Movement is powerful. We are in an age now where we use our mind so much more than our bodies. We are constantly on our computers and on our phones. We are occupied with moving forward with our careers, families, goals, and visions.

We have forgotten that our power is in using our whole body.

If you have become disconnected from this power, you can find it again only when you are in integrity. Movement is a vehicle to reconnect yourself to your body and your power. You can use this powerful tool to move your life forward in ways that are unimaginable.

The Power of Breath

Often overlooked, the breath can be one of the most powerful ways to transform your life.

Are you aware of how the breath works?

As babies, we are born breathing with our whole bodies. I really find that amazing.

Think about it. The way that you used to breathe was with your whole body. Of course, you no longer do that. As you grew up, you lost that ability, just as you lost that natural essence in movement and in life.

How did it change?

Our breaths get cut shorter over time. Under stress, we became conditioned to breathing in a different way, only using our lungs. We lose that whole-body breath. However, I believe we continue to have untapped potential in this area. Go deep with your breath and take it into your whole body. You can still strive to be in presence with the duality of your breath, in and out within yourself.

Go Deep

I use the breath as a tool for going deep. When my breath is in harmony with my body, it feels amazing. Like anyone, I sometimes lose that awareness. It is wonderful to feel the sensation of the power coming back to my body when I use my breath.

Slow your breath down and practice going deep within, with your breath. This idea is related to going deep within yourself when you are doing your inner work on personal beliefs.

This past year, I went to a *Tony Robbins: Unleashing the Power Within* event. My father had passed some months before, and I had worked on coming to terms with my grief and some issues we had had in our relationship. At that point, I felt that I had completely resolved those issues and was at peace with his passing, although I missed him and wished he was still a part of my life in physical form.

At this event, I realized that I had an important unresolved issue with my father that I had been unaware of until that day.

My father and I were really close growing up, but we lost that connection when I was a teenager. It wasn't a horribly bad experience, but the relationship between a father and son could be really powerful, and that was missing for me. When this realization came to the surface at this event, I felt it intensely. Tony was leading the crowd through a visualization technique with eyes closed when I had this realization. I was stunned.

I realized that I had been trying to make up for this relationship by attempting to be somebody important. I was trying to fill the void I felt inside by being successful.

I was wearing a hat that day, as I had gotten into the habit of doing. My hair was thinning and I felt self-conscious about it, but I hadn't admitted this to myself. When I got home from that event, I shaved my hair, the little hair that I had.

As a result, I felt like a powerful new me. This result, the outer result, was due to my inner work. I had gone deep within to seek the truth about my feelings about my father and about myself.

Go deep. This is what I want to stress.

We try so hard to make changes on the outside, often without doing the deep inner work. No matter what changes you make on the outside, you won't feel fulfilled if you don't do the inner work. If you focus on going deep within yourself and doing the work, the outer will be easy — truly, it will be.

It is the natural way of things. Take a deep breath and pay attention to the way it happens: First, you go deep within your breath and then you — naturally — breathe out.

Power is found in going deep. Everything is connected at the deepest level. Go deep, do the work, and find the harmony. It is waiting for you.

The breathing process involves a duality, an input and an output. We need to acknowledge both and put them into balance. Body movements have a similar duality. Dropping down is the input and the output is the expansion forward. We need to acknowledge both these elements and put them into balance, just like breathing.

OPEN UP AND RUN YOUR OWN RACE

When you have begun to master the process of moving your body in a way that embodies your natural essence, it will free you to be who you are.

You will begin to understand the *maxim of freedom*.

Simply stated: *You are free to be who you are.*

It is time to open up and run your own race.

Don't be afraid. If you are fearful, you will be running someone else's race. All your actions will be directed by what others are doing.

We want to move faster, we want to move up in the world, we want to be more successful than so-and-so, and we get into this space of not being true with ourselves. We run other people's races, and we don't even know we are doing that.

If you start running your own race as an individual and being with your own self, think about how powerful that can be. You will be in harmony with yourself, and that will radiate out to others. Powerful change can happen once you start running your own race.

Going Through the Full Range of Motion

When I was a sprinter, going through the full range of motion in my stride was one of the hardest things to do, but it is one of the most valuable training techniques. If you can go through the full range of motion as fast and loose as you possibly can, you will be generating your highest speed and power.

If you are an athlete, you will try to perfect or correct your course of movement for the techniques that matter to you most.

Some sample movements an athlete might be working on are listed below:

- The pitching motion in baseball or softball
- The lay-up in basketball
- The instep foot pass in soccer
- Swinging a bat or a golf club
- The running motion for sprinters
- A back handspring in gymnastics
- The long jump in track and field

It is vital for your training that, no matter which motion you're working on, you concentrate on going through *the full range of motion.* If you are not an athlete, it is still beneficial to your body to use the full range of motion for any physical movements, from walking to swimming to yoga.

When I was a sprinter, this technique was extremely helpful to me. However, as I said, it was one of the hardest things I ever did. When you start training yourself to go through the full range of motion, it will feel awkward when all you want is to feel smooth. It will feel like it is slowing you down, when all you want to do is speed up. Don't give up!

Training yourself to go through a full range of motion when you are working on any skill gives you the opportunity to fully apply forces downward — to put that foot down. It will help you to generate power. When you can harness that power, your techniques will be faster, stronger, and more efficient.

For runners, speed is the result of how fast the stride is moving and how long the stride is. The full range of motion allows the body to generate more power down towards the ground resulting in a longer stride length — which equals more speed.

What happens when you cut your range of motion short?

You lose power. I know that I did this many times in races. Usually, it was the result of being in fear mode, because I was behind in a race, or because I was worried about getting behind. It felt like I wasn't running fast enough, and to run faster, I cut short my range of motion.

This happens in your movements through life as well. I see it often in others and in myself, too. It works the same way I described above; when you cut short your range of motion in life, you lose power.

For instance, you might cut your range of motion in your relationships short, because you are impatient and want to move faster. In business, you might take a shortcut because you feel you are not progressing fast enough; this is like cutting short your range of motion. You might be focused so strongly on one part of your life that you let other parts drift aimlessly. This is another way of not using your full range of motion. All parts of your life are related and will affect the others.

Using your full range of motion feels like you are moving slower. You might feel like you're not getting anywhere, but you really are. If you want to go from point A to point B as fast as you can, you need to go through your full range of motion. It is going to feel slower, but your motion will be much more powerful.

Whether you are an athlete or not, use your full range of motion. Trust it to get you where you need to go.

Open Spaces

If you are not running your own race, then you are not going through the full range of motion. Conversely, if you are going through the full range of motion, then you are running your own race.

When you go through the full range of motion, your body creates wide open spaces. Visualize this. You can see the open spaces between your legs, between the separation of your arms and in your body. It makes athletes look bigger than they actually are.

Picture someone running like this, using the full range of motion, and creating big open spaces: Can you see that they look joyful, like the child on the track that Coach Tellez told me to look at?

You, too, can start looking like that again. Moving your body with these fully open spaces will ignite a sense of joy. In life, you can also become joyful when you use your full range of motion. Generating these open spaces will help you to move through life with more ease and happiness. When I shaved my hair, for example, this action was a demonstration of moving with my full range of motion. I never knew how much I would love myself and this look. It felt so good.

Reach out and use your full range of motion in all parts of your life. The wide-open places you create will become openings through which you'll attract other people. The open spaces promote creativity, are naturally magnetizing, and they tend to multiply. You will start opening the doors within your own self to attract what it is you need, and to help others with what they need as well. You will be able to serve each other, and that feels good.

When I see athletes move their bodies, I look at their open spaces. When an athlete is moving through their full range of motion, the fully open spaces are easy to see. You can sense how joyous they are when they move and when they perform.

When I see a person like this, I think: *This person has it.*

Whether they also have it in life, I can't be sure, but I know that they could take those open spaces and bring them into their lives as well.

When I see these people, I want to remind them: *What you can do on the field or on the court, you can do in life as well.*

That is part of the work I do with all my clients.

I remind them: *You must go deep.*

When you are training, don't just work superficially. I won't work superficially with my clients. If you choose to stay superficial, you can still go get in shape so you perform amazingly. You might feel like you are successful, but it won't last. You might have it on the court, but you won't have it in life. If you only do the output work—the outer work, the surface work—you will only have temporary results. I urge you to go deep.

I had to do that deep work in order for me to feel this way. If I had taken the superficial road, I could still have gone into the training world. I could be providing a temporary fix—a Band-Aid—to clients. I feel certain I would still have a void within me if I had gone that way. It would have been reflected somewhere in my physical presence and today, I would be incomplete and unfulfilled. Go deep.

Expect the Surge

When you can go through the full range of motion and feel the open spaces in your body, acknowledge how you look. Notice how beautiful you look and how much joy there is in feeling those open spaces when you move your body.

Be conscious of these feelings whether you are doing a run, a power walk, or lunges. Be conscious of the spaces opening in your physical body and in life. Sense the opening of doors as you jog or walk. Feel the difference as you do high-intensity work or aerobics. Sense the new freedom you possess.

Soon, you will have sensations that make you think: *Wow, I know something good is coming.*

You are about to experience what I call *the surge.* You will be able to feel it when it comes to you.

Here are some of the signs:

- Expect the surge when you know that what you are doing is not moving only your body, but moving it in a way that is harmonious with everything.

- When the surge is happening, things will start clicking in all parts of your life: in exercise, in your career, in your relationships.

- You will be feeling joyous and you will know that more goodness is coming.

- Opportunities will come to you without effort.

- You will feel free, egoless, and full of potential all at the same time.

- The surge comes when you have become an open vessel, and divinity will be moving through you.

The surge happens when you get into the zone that I call *the field of possibilities*. The body is the tool you use to get to this zone. If you are not there yet, it is coming. When you are aware that what is happening in your life is part of being in that zone, the experience is all the more powerful.

Sometimes, negative incidents happen. You may not always be throwing the best pitches, but this is all part of the process. Have faith. You have the capacity to get into that field where everything flows in your favor. We all do. No matter what you do, whether you are an athlete, a writer, or an actor, you have the field within you. You just need to access it.

You've probably heard professional athletes and coaches refer to *the zone* when they're talking about athletic performance. Many have tried to figure out how athletes can get into that zone.

Why can certain athletes find the zone while others can't?

Why do some find the zone only once, but can't ever find it again?

Michael Jordan said when he was in that zone, it felt as if the basketball hoop was wider. In my experience, when I was in the zone, I never thought about the finish line. I was fully in the experience of the moment. It was a timeless space.

During the race at USC that I talked about in an earlier chapter, I was in that zone. I didn't know what I did to get there; it just happened. I tried many years after that to duplicate it, even when I wasn't competing. That day, I didn't even know who I would be running against, and it didn't matter. I was truly connected to something greater. Afterwards, I'd continually watch the recording of that race and would wonder what I did to get in that zone. I couldn't duplicate it for a long time afterward.

The problem was that I was trying too hard. The best athletes allow the performance to come to them instead of them trying to go to it. I tried to force it, and it will never come like that. The surge always comes when you are not trying to find it. You are just in it. There is a deep sense of connection to yourself and everything. At the same time, you are detached from your mind. Your focus is not so much on the performance but on that deep connection. There is no great performance without a deep sense of connection.

Once I started to apply my own training system, which was born from doing my own personal belief work, I started to understand there is a way to get back to that zone, the field of possibilities. It's not the way that I had thought it would be. You can only get there by being truly present with your body and your movement.

It is all in the application of the eight principles of my method. So far, we have discussed the first six in detail: Ground, Gravity, Integrity, Joy, Harmony, and Freedom. The last two—Now and Action—will be talked about in the next chapters.

Once I could apply these principles to my own body, and in my own life, I was finally able to find the zone again in another race. That brought me so much joy. I knew then that I had something special to share with the world.

These maxims are virtues we embody as children, but lose as we grow older. You lose connection to them once you are less in your body and more in your head.

It is possible that our schools don't emphasize the importance of the body-mind connection enough and are more focused on the memorization of material that only scratches the surface of our intelligence. I see a future where physical education is more about preserving our natural movement and learning how it can be harnessed for joy, fulfillment, and long-term health.

Besides finding the zone for my body, I found it in life, too. You are reading this book because I wrote it from the field of possibilities. It isn't a place that you can stay in without work, however. I am continually challenged. Life throws me curve balls every now and then, but I am able to see what's coming. I can maneuver through these experiences and close the gap.

Once, during a Landmark Forum event in Los Angeles, I participated in a visualization exercise. During the session, a fear of mine unexpectedly came up. I was unaware of it because it was deep seated within my subconscious, but it was affecting my choices in life.

Kids used to play football and baseball in the street when I was a kid. I was a natural athlete growing up and I scored many touchdowns and runs in these street games. This was just how I was. It was natural for me.

A couple days after one game in which I had done well, I was walking back from the school bus stop. It was about a half-mile walk from the bus to my home. There was a boy walking across the street. I recognized him — he had been in that same game but on the other team. I saw that he made a turn and started walking behind me. I didn't think anything of it. He got close to me and tapped my shoulder. As I was turning around, he took a swing and knocked me out.

When I came back to consciousness, he was gone. I was confused. I didn't understand what had happened. My mind hid that experience from me.

As an adult, when that experience came back, it was overwhelming to become fully aware of it again. I had many questions.

Why had my mind hidden it from me?

Why did it come back?

Why did I need to think about it now?

After some thought, I discovered that I had a belief hidden inside me and it was associated with that childhood memory. There was a part of me that felt succeeding in life would result in being hit the way I was that day. As a result, I lived my life staying small, trying not to achieve too much. I tried not to be too much better than anyone for fear of embarrassing someone. I believed that if I was truly myself and was successful at doing what I did, that I would be knocked down.

We all have experiences like that. You may hide yours deep inside so that they can only come to the surface when you do deep inner work. Working with the body is an opportunity for you to start this work. You are not your beliefs. There are people out there — therapists and other life coaches — to help you look at your deep-seated fears and the belief systems that go with them.

If you can't see the beliefs that are driving your life, then you are not truly running your own race. You are running someone else's race, and that is a fear-based mentality instead of a love-based mentality.

Run your own race.

CHAPTER FOUR

The Connection Between Body, Life, and Environment

GET BACK TO THE BASICS

To make the kinds of changes we've been talking about so far, you must get back to the basics. Your body, your breath, your awareness, your life experience, and your relationships will all be a part of the equation. These are the basics elements available to you to help you make fundamental changes in your life.

Athletes

Athletes traditionally have a very linear way of thinking. They set goals and are very determined and motivated to reach their goals. They desire the shortest path between where they are and where their goal is. I had that same mentality. This kind of self-motivation is a powerful intangible force.

When I was in high school, I was the first Mexican-American to win the hundred-meter sprint in the California Interscholastic Federation (CIF) Southern Section. But even then, when I applied to Cal State Long Beach, I didn't initially get a spot on the team.

To get accepted into the university required a great deal of effort on my part. My own motivation had to carry me because I didn't have parental support or guidance in that area. In my family, just graduating high school meant you were successful. Going higher than that was new territory.

On my own, I filled out the applications and I was able to get into Cal State Long Beach, but I couldn't run my freshman year. According to the state's Proposition 48, my SAT scores didn't meet the requirements to play a sport for Cal State my first year. I had to focus on my academics and prove myself first.

I was determined to get on the track and field team, so I worked hard on my studies that first year. Eventually, I was able to get on the team.

When I finally had the opportunity to meet with the head coach in person, I said to him, "My picture is going to be up on your wall one day."

I had the confidence and the motivation to meet my goals. Without self-motivation, I never would have gotten on the team. Nothing external can push you as effectively. Motivation is an inside job.

It is ingrained in an athlete's mentality to move with force and determination, focusing only on the goal. However, as you have already read, this kind of approach can result in superficial results and a persistent lack of fulfillment in athletics and in life.

Training with The Hart Method requires that athletes change this mentality, which is sometimes difficult. I make it clear to them that I'm not a coach in the traditional sense. I tell them that what I'm trying to do is to help them unlearn everything they have learned along the way.

Once they successfully put their foot down and they feel the difference in their body, they are often amazed. They express regret that they didn't make these changes sooner.

I hear them say things like, "What have I been doing all this time?"

For athletes, I focus on the drills that every athlete knows — universal drills like *high-knees*, and the *a-skip*. This gives them the ability to strive for optimum movement using drills they are already familiar with, and to feel the difference when they use my techniques.

Fitness Enthusiasts

Besides working with professional athletes, I work with fitness enthusiasts of all levels.

How do I help these non-professionals improve their movements?

There are a multitude of different fitness programs out there right now and clients often come to me after having tried a variety of them. Many of these programs are high-intensity, and they emphasize a mentality of overcoming pain by using grit, and forcing the body for results. I cringe every time I see this, or when I see instructors or coaches who do not have the awareness of how to move the body in a healthy, efficient way. I believe that these programs do more harm than good. In addition, they do not even come close to harnessing the true power of the body.

With fitness enthusiasts, I do universal exercises such as the lunge, the step-up, and stair climbing. I try to show them that little shifts in movement can make drastic changes in the body. Any movement—power walking, running, aerobics, and dance, for example—can be an opportunity to put the foot down and start feeling optimal changes in your body. Moving with the maxims will help your body to remember, and then you can carry those changes into your life.

Everyday People

If you are reading this book and thinking to yourself: *I'm not into working out, I'm not a fitness enthusiast, and I'm not an athlete. How can I use this method?*

I met someone the other day who said, "I have trouble doing anything physical. I am a very spiritual person. I have my life goals. I am very determined and motivated in that way, but I don't have this connection with my body. I don't work out. I don't do anything."

I asked her, "Do you walk?"

She said, "Well, yes."

I said, "Let's start with that. Let's start with looking at *how* you walk. When you walk, you are most likely thinking only about moving the legs forward. Embody a sense of balance by acknowledging that there is also back action. You will feel it once your mind knows it. One leg going back while the other is going forward is harmonious. This will ignite a more confident, bouncier walk. It's simple but powerful as you incorporate this awareness to life. Forward movement is a result of going back or down as well. I recommend walking barefoot on the earth to connect deeply with yourself and environment."

Perhaps you want to live a better life than you are right now. Maybe you want to change the world. You can start by changing how you walk.

Try walking this way:

- Loosen your shoulders.

- Move your leg back while feeling the ground and simultaneously move the other leg forward. Feel the momentum.

- Feel the bounce every time you take a step.

- Be conscious of your breath.

- Move the arms through the full range of motion.

- When you're walking, try to get a sense of your own strength and freedom.

- Find your way to being in the moment.

- Feel your body, be one with your movement, and visualize your goals. The simple movements involved with walking can help you feel a connection with your core.

LIFE IS YOUR FORCE

Life is your force. It is the here and now, and it is all yours—your relationships, your experience, and your challenges. Right at this moment, you have a multitude of opportunities to move your life forward. It's not magical; it's just life. Your force is here for you to harness it and move forward.

Life Will Be Life

Having a goal or intention is not optional; it is necessary. When you put your intentions out into the universe, you give yourself an opportunity to grow. For example, I put out the intention of writing this book so I could share the messages you are reading about. Life gave me the opportunity to make this happen.

Life, of course, doesn't necessarily give you all positive experiences. It gives you what you need. Don't close your heart when you have difficult times. Instead, open your heart and your awareness to allow life to come in, no matter what is happening.

When you have set a goal, send it out and imagine life saying to you: *You have this goal or this intention. OK. Let me give you what you need — not what you think you need — but exactly what you need in order to move forward.*

Life will give you exactly what you need, both negative and positive. Don't get caught up in either of these. Stay balanced. If you get too high or too low, you will lose your focus.

Don't act out of fear. Fear will make you cut your movement short or try to avoid it completely. Fear makes you close your heart to experiences. You will limit your possibilities if you act out of fear. You may even stop moving forward altogether.

Don't expect your path to be straight. You may have unexpected twists and turns in your path and you might be tempted to hold back. You might think something is wrong when your path isn't as straight as you imagined. It might even seem like you are moving backward instead of forward. Have faith that life is giving you what you need.

Remember, you need to put your foot down in order for the body to move up and forward. When you put your foot down, you apply down-and-back forces to move forward. When you are using a bow and arrow, you need to pull the bow *back* in order for the arrow to shoot *forward*. The arrow shooting forward toward the target can't happen unless you have the awareness of the need to pull backwards. Life works in the same way.

Life will be life. You need to have a clear mind during those slumps or difficult times. The piano has dark keys for a reason. The song has moments of silence for a reason. We have storms for a reason. You must understand that those moments are a part of your process and you must stay present in these moments.

Be aware and conscious so you can move your life forward. Life is a force. It will be there for you. Believe.

Grow for It

Grow for it is a saying that I love. It embodies a feeling of self-motivation, and combines this with the intention of growth.

Go for it is more commonly heard, and it invokes a very different mentality. It also has a feeling of self-motivation, but without a balanced intention.

We all need to be self-motivated. But sometimes, you get caught up in going for something without having a balance of input and output. Sometimes, you may get caught up in forcing your body to move forward, in forcing goals to happen.

In order to move forward in a way that expands your possibilities, you need to grow. That is where life comes in. That is where experiences come in. It is about going back to the basics and getting opportunities to grow authentically. In growing for it, you may achieve something that you could not have imagined.

In my own experience, I had the mentality of going for it, and when I went for it, without being balanced within myself, I achieved my goal, but it didn't feel good. I broke records due to determination, and it only gave me happiness for a little while; I needed to accomplish something else to have that sense of happiness once again. There was no real fulfillment.

But when I started to engage with myself, I became more self-aware and was able to chase away the self-limiting beliefs I had. I opened my heart up to all of life's experiences, and I became a more balanced man.

Growing for it was much more fulfilling than *going for it*. It still is.

Allowing Versus Forcing

In the body, those downward forces that I keep talking about can be harnessed to move you forward. If you trust in this process and stay in the moment, you can align your body to receive these forces, and allow them to carry your body forward. It is all about *allowing*, not *forcing*.

If you are an athlete, this mentality will enable the performance to come to you instead of you forcing yourself to perform. Athletes at the top of their game harness this kind of power and allow it to work for them. The power simply flows. This is when great performances arise.

In life, this same concept applies. Be present and trust in your process and the goodness that life has to offer will come to you. It starts with the body. It starts by simply putting the foot down. For me, that is the first step in making these drastic changes. Putting the foot down opens up a whole new world of possibilities where everything flows.

Be aware that the divinity you embody will give you what you need. We all want beautiful things in life, and we think that they will come wrapped with bows and pretty decorations. In your head, you may think that your intentions should look a certain way. In my experience, my own being gave me what I needed, but it didn't always look the way I saw it in my mind.

When you start this process, keep a deep sense of gratitude for what you have right here, and right now. Trust that it is exactly what you need to move forward.

ONE MOVEMENT

Humanity has a desire to feel oneness. I think that is our true intention as a collective. We want to be in harmony with each other. Your experiences in the world can help you grow, and help you reach this kind of harmony. Just as we go through challenging experiences to grow as individuals, we also have experiences that help us to move forward as one collective.

How do you reach this kind of harmony?

Here are some thoughts that can help you begin:

- Harmony comes from inside you. This may be hard to believe, but inside each of us is a natural, powerful force that can affect the world around us.

- Without engaging this inner force, any changes that you make will be very superficial. Remember that moving your body without connecting to your inner essence — without putting your foot down — is ineffective and superficial.

- Superficial changes in life, just as in your body, will be ineffective and short-lived.

- We see this every day, in national and world politics. Making real change requires going deep, and it is difficult, but it is the only way to achieve oneness in the world. I am convinced it is possible.

You have your own way of seeking this oneness. We are all different. My mission is to get people to move their bodies joyously and harmoniously once again, to feel that oneness and freedom within themselves, within their body and their lives, and then to radiate out that oneness to their environment, and from the environment to the world.

One of my life goals is to someday harness the power of corporations and collaborate with celebrity types — from actors to athletes — to spread this message to the masses. We need to remind the multitude that we all have the capacity to reignite transformation from the inside out.

Inner Change Creates Outer Results

Implode to explode: This is a kind of imagery that I use in training my clients.

I am not a scientist; I have never done any scientific research on how this universe was created, but I have learned about the Big Bang. The Big Bang was the result of an implosion that created an explosion. It could have happened simultaneously and it may be still happening.

Consider the way body movements work, as we've talked about in previous chapters. As the forces are being applied down and back, opposite forces are moving up and forward. My inner knowledge tells me that this is also how the universe works; it tells me that what works for the body also works for the universe.

The body is a microcosm of the macrocosm. It is a reflection of the grand universe. It follows that if you can make a change within your own body, then you can make a change in the world.

As a child, a connection with your natural essence was your birthright. You embodied a sense of balance between input and output, between masculine and feminine, between dark and light. It was all there — and the potential is still there. The path back to that state is in the unlearning of everything you absorbed along the way. For this reason, much of my method involves finding ways of *un-teaching* my clients.

Trust in that potential. It is still there.

You Are Part of the Whole

The body is an interconnected network of parts, as we've discussed before. When one body part is out of harmony, then the whole body is out of harmony. In the same way, when one person is out of harmony and doesn't feel that they are one within themselves, then the whole collective is affected.

We are all connected; it always comes back to that. Since every individual is part of the whole, every individual is important. We are all separate parts, but there is an unbreakable connection.

When you are an athlete, the connection between your body parts can be obvious. A broken pinky — or even a hangnail on your pinky — can affect your performance. As a sprinter, I knew that every tiny injury was a risk. Even having a hangnail was risky because the body would compensate for it and sometimes, this would cause an injury.

I used to wonder: *How can something so small have a big effect?*

We all have that kind of connection to the whole. You are connected to the whole of humanity. If you are aware of this, it will change your approach to your own life. You matter. You count. By maximizing your own life, you can radiate that to others and inspire others to also connect to themselves.

Do you want to help the world, improve the environment, or change a political system?

Instead of trying to force change on the outside, start with yourself.

In my lifetime, there have been some amazing developments in our world — in technology, in individual perceptions, and in world consciousness — and I believe we are getting closer to having our needs met. I am not one of those who believes that humanity is getting worse.

Yes, we have challenges to overcome, but we have all the tools for change available to us. The answers are close to home; the power is right inside you, and the shift is simple.

The World Moves

Sometimes, we forget the world is continually moving and that it is a living being. It's turning—moving forward, moving back—and it is breathing. When I remind myself of the natural movement of the world, I feel like an important part of that movement.

Our world is constantly changing its position in the universe. This is a reminder for me to continually move my position, and not to get stagnant or stuck in a routine.

Continually move and change your routine, keeping yourself aware of the way your body is meant to move. This starts with putting your foot down, and connecting with the maxims of ground, gravity, integrity, joy, harmony, freedom, the power of now, and action. Embody those principles and know that your natural way of moving your body is connected to the continual movement of the world. We can get humanity to move with the world and to move together in harmony.

It all starts with creating that movement within your own self and your own individual life.

When I was an athlete, I found it such a challenge to give of myself to anything else besides my sport. I felt like if I gave too much time to my girlfriend or to my family or to anything else, it would take away from the goals that I had as an athlete. This was my mentality. You can see that it was fear-based.

When I did give to another, it wasn't authentic. It was something I felt like I had to do, and this approach built resentment. Once I started to put my foot down, and I started to work on myself, a whole new world opened up for me. I started to see that putting my foot down was a form of giving. The opposite leg coming forward and up was a form of receiving.

Giving and receiving work hand in hand, and it's not only about other people. You also need to start giving to yourself. Become aware that putting the foot down is a form of giving to yourself, of coming back to your power, and back to the natural way of moving your body.

Once you can do that with your body, you can do it in life. You can give to others in an authentic way. You will find that giving to others is a way of receiving as well. When I think of giving, I think of the power of being generous. The word *generous* itself reminds us of the word *generate*. To generate is to produce. So in reality, when I am generous I am manifesting. It's a win-win!

When you embrace this understanding, the action of putting your foot down goes even deeper. It is an action of giving down to the earth. You deepen your connection to your planet, to your home. Take your shoes off and feel this connection. It's healing.

For me, if something works in the body, then it works in life. For me, writing this book is a form of giving. I am also receiving. It's like a secret blessing. Whenever there is an opportunity for me to give and it feels good, then I know I am receiving at the same time.

This may be a fundamental change in your way of thinking. You may think of giving as involving a loss of something. Even though you may be glad that it makes someone else happy, it still feels like something is taken away from you. That's not true.

When I had my first child, my boy, I had this belief that if I had a child, it would take away from my life and my career goals. I thought I had gotten over that belief years before, but it was still there. I feared that having a child might take away from my life and my career. It might interfere with my training philosophy and the plans I had to write a book.

I had a conversation with myself.

I asked myself: *Why do you have this fear? Aren't you finished with that fear-based mentality?*

I reminded myself: *You talk about giving and receiving, and you believe in that. Have faith.*

After this conversation, I fully gave myself to having a child, and it has been such a blessing. It added so much richness to my life and it has brought so many other things to me. It changed *everything*.

It was a miracle for me—I *gave life* to this amazing boy! He could be the reason why I am writing this book and why it has solidified to the point where it is now. We will always have challenges. Life will be life. Remind yourself not to be afraid to give. Put your foot down and feel the power of giving and receiving.

CHAPTER FIVE

The Power Is Here and Now

THE FUTURE IS HERE

Sometimes, we get caught up in—and I am talking from a personal perspective—either thinking about the past or worrying about the future, forgetting that the real power is in *the now*, which is the seventh maxim of The Hart Method.

You always have the ability and the capacity to reconnect yourself to the now. In truth, the now is all there is. If we harness the natural essence of the now, we can make some drastic changes not just in the present, but in the future as well, and not only as individuals, but also as a collective humanity.

Past, Present, and Future

Whenever I hear those words together, I remember the day I had a life-changing realization. I went for a jog on a beach. Usually, when I move my body, a kind of meditation is involved. On this day, I started off sitting in a still position, focusing on my breath and trying to keep my awareness with my breath and my body. Then I took that awareness with me to my moving body, meditating and staying present while I was jogging and thinking about the maxims of my training philosophy. I kept repeating the principles to myself starting with *ground* and *putting my foot down*, feeling the earth on my feet, and being aware of how my body felt, feeling the power of putting my foot down. From there, I moved through the other maxims, as we have discussed in previous chapters.

On that run, I had a magical realization.

I remember saying to myself: *Just put your foot down. Put your foot down.*

I felt the down motion, and then there was this back movement, which was my leg going back. Then there was the forward movement of the opposite leg going forward.

I started thinking: *Down, back, and forward. Down, back, and forward.*

Repeating this, it soon became just one word in my mind: *Downbackandforward.*

It started with *the down*, which I had come to learn is the same as *the now*. Down, back, and forward became *the now, present, and future.*

I started to see that as one word as well: *Nowpresentandfuture*.

Suddenly, I could see it all clearly. It was all an expansion of the now. In reality, the essence of life — and the only essence — is the now. Where I am and how I am able to harness this now is what creates my future. In addition, whatever changes my future is also changing my past in some way. This natural essence, this magical now, can open the possibilities to some magical future but also somehow changes the past.

That is how the power of the now came to me. Notice that this all happened through my body. There is a natural ability in all of us to harness the power of the now. The vehicle for that process is your very own body.

Take Off the Blinders

Blinders are pieces of leather attached to a horse's bridle to prevent the horse from seeing behind and to the side. If you are only looking at your goal and nothing else, you are, in effect, wearing blinders.

You need to take them off.

Visualize a racehorse with blinders on, focusing on the endpoint and running as fast as he can. There is a reason why we do that to a horse. We want him to get to the finish line faster than every other horse, and we don't want him distracted by his environment.

In the introduction, I told the story of bumping into Misty May-Treanor, two-time Olympic gold medalist in beach volleyball. But there's more to my experience with Misty May. I had run into her twice at random spots before our car wash experience. I feel that the universe was showing me my true path, but because of my blinders, I failed to see it. Possibilities hover all around us, but we will fail to see them if we're more connected to our egos than being in touch with the wholeness of our being.

Taking your blinders off gives you the chance to fully see yourself and to reconnect with your power, with the essence of yourself. It gives you the opportunity to connect with your whole essence, with your whole entire being, not just body, but mind, spirit, and environment.

Remember the fear-based mentality of the runner focusing on his trail leg?

When you are focused on the trail leg behind you, and not on the leg right beneath you, you are focusing on the past. You are not in the now.

When you put on blinders, the same kind of problem exists; you are only focused on the end of the race; you are not in the now. You are trying to create a future from your past. You are going from point A to B as fast as you can, trying to get there faster than everyone else. In doing so, you are risking your fulfillment, your body, and your health.

Taking off the blinders will give you a whole new perspective. It will open up a whole new world of possibilities for you, from B to C, D, E, F, G, H, to Z, and beyond—to letters and sounds that are not yet in your alphabet.

Focusing only on future goals, instead of on the present, is a common problem that I see in both athletes and non-athletes. It is ineffective for both. When you do this, you are carrying your past into your future. It is fear-based and extremely limiting, for your body and your life. As you move into the future, you will be bringing your past baggage with you, whether you know it or not.

When you have this kind of problem, your thoughts might be like these:

Why does this always happen to me?

Why do I always attract the same kind of partner?

Why do I always end up in the same kind of unsatisfying job?

If these are your thoughts, you can be sure that there is something you are bringing from your past into your future.

We can also be following the same kind of pattern as a culture, or as a nation, or as humanity.

What are we, as humans, bringing from our past into our future?

Does it sometimes seem like history is repeating itself?

This happens when we bring our past into the future instead of focusing on fixing the present. I see this everywhere now. We keep ending up in the same place.

We have the potential to see this, to understand it, and ultimately, to fix it. There is a way we can do that. My ultimate dream is to have a world in which we can talk about our beliefs and harness our power to make the world better. History doesn't actually repeat itself because no two experiences are alike. However, I believe the opportunity for change will repeat until we choose to take action.

Going From A to B

Twenty years ago, my passion was running the hundred-meter sprint. There was a starting point — A, and there was the ultimate finish line — B. My goal was to get from point A to B as fast as I could, so I put on blinders and tried to move my body as fast as I could from A to B.

Now, I realize that there are other ways of thinking about racing. There are methods and principles I could have applied that would have opened up possibilities for me.

Here are two questions for you about points A and B:

Where was I when I started those races?

Where was my focus?

I was at A. But my focus was entirely on B — the finish line. I had taken the focus completely away from myself.

However, my real power could only be found by putting the focus on A, on me, in the moment. Then, whatever I did with my body, what I did with myself in the moment, was what would eventually create B. Changing my mentality took work — it is easier said than done — but it is what I had to do to access my power.

In life, the same idea applies. For me, when I started to put the focus on A, on me in the moment, it gave me the ability to get to B. Not only did it get me to B, but B changed along the way into a whole new world of possibilities. That is the reason why I am here writing this book.

When I put the focus on A, on myself, B opened up into the writing of this book. If I had put my focus on the production of a book from the beginning, and put myself to the side, I think my possibilities would have been limited. If I had been able to finish the book under those circumstances, I am certain the results would have been limited. It wouldn't have brought the fulfillment that it is bringing me now.

BEING THE ZERO

If you imagine a number line, where is point A on that line?

We know A is at the beginning, at the starting line. Therefore, A is found at the zero of the number line. That means that zero is where I am in the present.

What does this mean?

Visualize the circle shape of the zero in your mind. That circle embodies your body, mind, and spirit. You have been conditioned to think the zero has no value, that only the numbers that indicate quantity have value. The value we all have as whole individuals, however, can be found in the zero.

You have been conditioned to think that fulfillment is something you achieve outside of yourself. Just as you are conditioned to believe that zero is nothing of value, you are conditioned to believe that being at point A has no value. You have been told that you are not good enough unless you can get to point B faster and better than everyone else.

Someone may ask, "Point B is just a goal, isn't it? What's wrong with having goals?"

There is nothing wrong with having goals. In fact, having them is recommended. You must develop a vision and put your goals out there in order for the universe to deliver what you need, as we discussed before.

The problem develops when you put your *complete focus* on that goal. This causes you to become separated from yourself. Fulfillment can't be found if you are separated from yourself. Your conquest becomes superficial, and any sense of success quickly fades away until you conquer another goal.

We have developed this same mentality toward goals of world change. We have become so absorbed in the desire to change the world that we have become disembodied from ourselves. We have become devoted to something external and cannot be in integrity with ourselves. In order to transcend, we must descend back into ourselves.

We must learn to return to ourselves and *be the zero* — be in the moment — once again.

The Number Line

When I imagine a number line, I see the zero in the middle as a *container of everything*. From the zero, there is an expansion of numbers in both directions. If all numbers from the positive are expanding from the zero to infinity, and on the other end, negative numbers expand to negative infinity, this means that the zero must be a container of everything. Zero has an ability to attract and magnetize into itself.

What does all of this mean for you?

- Zero has the value of now, just like your whole, complete body.

- You have the same potential to expand outward, to create, and to magnetize. Acknowledge that in yourself.

- Don't describe your value in what you create, but value yourself no matter what you create, whether it's positive or negative.

- Your value is not in the past or present, but in the moment.

- Don't attach yourself to your accomplishments; they are not your identity.

- Your identity is who you are, and that's in the now, in the zero.

- Who you are in your body and spirit, your whole complete self, is your power and your true, authentic value.

Positive and Negative

So, the zero is now. That's all there is. Everything is an expansion of that.

The positive and the negative are also relatable to the future and the past. The positive represents the future, and all your potential and possibilities. The negative is a representation of the past.

The past and the future are just two directions from the zero point; they are neither good nor bad. Sometimes, you may see your past as a negative part of yourself. You may sometimes get caught up in the future, in dreams or fear. You may think too much about the past or feel anxiety about the future. Instead, be in the zero—that is who you are.

It's easy to get caught up in those experiences and use them to create an identity, but it won't really reflect who you are. You are not your experiences, whether they are good or bad. Your identity is who you are at your core, and your true power is in the here and now.

As I often tell my athletes: *Come back to yourself.*

I am talking about the zero point. The zero point is you. Don't think about the outcome; think about what is happening right now with your body and your movements.

If you have a bad performance, don't get caught up in that. Don't get too high or too low. Come back to yourself — that is where your power lies. You can open up a whole new world of possibilities, where you may exceed your best performance. Your performance, after all, is a result of how connected you are to yourself.

A song is like a performance; it is a creation. In a song, there is real power in the spaces where there is no sound, where there is silence. You can feel the power in the silent build-up to what's coming. This is especially true if you know the song; you can feel what's coming from that space of nothingness.

The space of nothingness creates what is heard in that next note or sound. Think about your career like that, whether you are an athlete or businessman. Whenever there is a down-slope or slump, there is an opportunity in front of you. Take that opportunity to become fully present with your process and be ready to create your next beautiful performance.

Maximize that space of nothingness. It may be hard to do, when you are losing races, getting no hits, or can't find the strike zone. Sometimes, that slump can last for a while, but you need to stay present and keep your mental attitude. The space of nothingness is necessary for that next great performance to come. Think of it as keeping the doors open to greatness. If you get caught up in fear and anger, you may be closing the doors to the greatness that is trying to creep through.

Being in the Zone: The Field of Possibilities

In these empty spaces, it may feel like nothing is working. Stay present, anyway — you will be giving yourself an opportunity to allow that great performance or perfect game to happen.

Remember the importance of the downward forces of the body. Remember that forward movement depends on going down, even falling down. It all comes back to putting your foot down. This is the first step for everything, the beginning of reprogramming your body and your mind so you can bring this awareness to life and reclaim your power.

For an athlete, this is what gives you the opportunity to get in *the zone*.

You will notice that, when athletes talk about being in the zone, they will say things like: *I don't know what I did. It just happened.*

It happens effortlessly. In the field of possibilities, everything happens effortlessly. When you are in that empty space, when it feels like nothing is working, you have to have an awareness that you may be right on the edge of a new opportunity.

Don't judge the empty space. When it feels like nothing is working, you may tend to act out of fear, judging the space. You may see it as broken and if you do, you may spend your energy desperately trying to fix it. This is true of sports performance and it also may be true in life. The more that you attach yourself to fixing things, the less aware you will be of the space you are in.

Take another approach instead. Acknowledge being in this space as a necessary experience for you. Know that you are increasing the chances of being in the zone, of experiencing this beautiful way of living, of attracting the beautiful things that are part of your nature. When you are present in that space of nothingness, where nothing is clicking, you may be about to open a door to the possibility of being in a zone where *everything* is clicking.

Being in the field of possibilities is being the zero. Being the zero has nothing to do with being positive or negative. It has nothing to do with the value of numbers and it is not materialistic. The real value is the zero, which is your own self — body, mind, and spirit. If you can harness that power, which is harnessing yourself, a whole new world of possibilities will become available to you.

TAKE ACTION

Taking action is the last maxim of The Hart Method.

It's the last maxim for a reason. In the past, in my own experience, I have taken action without having self-awareness. This was a mistake.

I thought: *Go get it; just do it and it will bring fulfillment and happiness.*

It didn't. It's like shooting an arrow without being fully present right before the shot. It's like getting to a destination without knowing how you got there, reaching your goals without being truly fulfilled, or getting straight A's without having any deep sense of knowledge.

The key is in how you take action. You can follow the maxims to prepare yourself.

- Apply the principle of *ground* by putting your foot down.

- Apply the principle of *gravity* by losing your fear of making mistakes, knowing that forward movement can't happen without falling, and trusting the ground to be there for support.

- Apply the principle of *integrity* by being whole and complete in your body.

- Feel the joy of movement in the moment according to the maxim of *joy*.

- See yourself in others, understanding that everything circles back to you according to the maxim of *harmony*.

- Feel the sense of *freedom* that applying the maxims gives to you. The freedom maxim also gives you the capacity to go through the full range of motion fearlessly.

- Feel the power of *now*, knowing that this moment is all there is.

- Now, it is time to prepare for *action*, the final maxim of The Hart Method.

Live your life embodying these maxims and take action from that starting point to find your power. But in order to take action effectively, you need to have an intention.

Intention

Take some time to consider your intentions before you take action.

What is your vision?

What is it you want to strive for?

Having an intention is powerful. Life will respond to that intention and will give you exactly what you need to move toward that vision or perhaps something even greater.

Many people have difficulty with setting goals and intentions. Let's say your goal is to lose thirty pounds. If you take action without the guiding principles you've already read about, you will limit the likelihood of achieving your goal and limit your possibilities in a larger sense. If you do reach your goal of losing the thirty pounds, you won't feel fulfilled.

Have a big vision, not a small one. If your vision is to lose thirty pounds, I recommend increasing it — lose the thirty pounds while decreasing six percent of your body fat. Add a bigger vision to that with these principles. A big vision will be more powerful for an individual to move forward and take action.

Have a big vision. Think about your whole life.

What is your ultimate vision as an individual?

What is our ultimate vision as a country, as a world?

When you have a big vision, everything that happens will become part of that vision. Take a new perspective. Become aware of the power of the big vision.

The Bow and Arrow

The bow and arrow is the perfect tool to demonstrate the concept of the big vision:

- To shoot an arrow, you need to pull the bowstring back to prepare.

- In the same way, you need a vision or intention before you can take action.

- To maximize the motion of the arrow, you can pull the bowstring back as far as possible. The more that you pull back, the faster that arrow is going to shoot forward.

- In the same way, to maximize your action, you need to have a big vision.

My wife and I married back in 2009 in Guatemala. We both decided to pack up and go after we had envisioned what our ceremony would look like. One day, I'd like to share my story, but suffice it to say that the result exceeded our vision. It was truly magical.

Seven years later, we renewed our vows at The Mission Inn in Riverside, California. Again, our ceremony exceeded our vision. All this was possible because we paused with awareness in making our decisions. We did not act in the fear of making mistakes and we remained present in the process. We remained playful, we enjoyed our environment, and we took focused action when necessary.

The connections I have been able to make on my journey have given me such a blessed life. My life has exceeded my expectations in so many ways, and now, I am further blessed because I can share what I have learned with others.

Taking Action With Natural Power

I have found something bigger than myself, and it all started with understanding my natural power through my body.

As a sprinter, my goal was to go from point A to point B as fast as possible. As a child, I knew the best way to get to point B was to not even think about point B. My childlike innocence didn't require reason or definitions. Movement was simply what it was. Children naturally exist in the moment.

As I grew older, I became conditioned to think that if I put all my focus on my goal, I could maximize my results. I was wrong. Although I achieved some success as a sprinter at the Division I level—I held school records in the hundred-meter and two-hundred-meter sprints for about twelve years at Cal State Long Beach—I believe that my potential was untapped.

I also had some success representing Mexico; I earned a bronze medal at the Pan American Games and was a two-time national champion in the hundred-meter race. In spite of my accomplishments, I was never truly fulfilled. I understand now that this was because my focus was entirely on superficial goals. As we have discussed in this chapter, instead of focusing on me, in the moment—point A—I was focused completely on the short-term goal—point B.

As an underground runner, I did find true fulfillment as a child, but once I got into my late teens, I lost that connection. I won many races but fulfillment was lost. I lost only two prize races—my first and my last.

Well, we come into this life crying and we leave crying, right?

What matters is how we lived it.

But the race that had the most impact was the most important one of them all.

After my leg injury in 1996, which kept me sidelined from competing at the Olympic Games, I went into a deep depression.

I was in a very dark place.

Any athlete will assure you that injuries are a good reason to be angry, sad, depressed, and to be a victim. During my road to recovery, as I've told you in previous chapters, I sought help from many sources. I went to Houston to train under Coach Tellez and I read books on biomechanics, spirituality, and self-help.

During this time, my dreams at night were vivid. Over and over, they made it clear to me that I was put on this planet for a reason. In one of my dreams, Jesus gave me seeds. In another dream, the goddess Shakti came out of my mid-section. I never considered myself very religious, but something or somebody was obviously trying to communicate with me.

I slowly began to reconnect the relationship between mind and body, and body and life. I started to feel the restoration of harmony in my life. I became aware that my dreams, my visions, and my potential were still within me. I felt a new sense of power even though I wasn't competing like I used to.

At this time, I was approached by the underground racing community. There was a new guy on the circuit making a killing, and I was invited to come back to race him. My first thought was to leave it alone and not get involved. But I had a feeling it was the right time to participate one more time, and then close the doors to this world and, perhaps, make room for something new. It felt like a ritual of sorts. I also wanted to put myself in a pressure situation in which the consequences of losing were high.

I took on the challenge. In this race, the wager exceeded one hundred fifty thousand dollars. All my people supported me and never doubted me. Some people bet against me, thinking I was beyond my prime. The other guy's fans were all people who had supported the opponents I had beaten in the past. They had always wanted to see me and my people lose, and they thought my time to lose had finally come.

This was my opportunity to put into practice The Hart Method. I had trained my body to move in the way that I used to when I'd run as a child — the way I ran against USC. This was my opportunity to feel that joy and freedom once again.

However, I had put myself in a high-pressure situation. Other people had risked a great deal of money on this race.

What if I lost?

Anything could happen in this underground world. People would do anything for money. One of my supporters told me that he had agreed to bet two thousand dollars, but he didn't actually have that money. If I lost, he would have been in big trouble. Others had wagered their savings, car, or their rent money.

Because of the pressure, I saw this race as an opportunity for me to practice my newly discovered realizations. In my preparation for the race, I moved my body with all the maxims of The Hart Method imprinted in my movements. In a quiet place, I visualized how these maxims felt in my body. I felt a deep sense of harmony between body and mind. It was as if my very cells were feeling the harmony. I visualized how these maxims could be carried over to my performance and, eventually, to my life. I visualized the outcome of the race in my head and throughout my whole body.

I knew I'd win even before the race. The feeling brought me a sense of joy. The race now felt more like a ritual in which I would put everything in motion. It would be a movement meditation that would set the tone for the next phase in my life. I practiced detachment and connection simultaneously, despite the pressure.

Right before the race, I rubbed earth from the track on my body. I looked up at the sun, and I smiled. I already had done all this. After the race, I was put up on shoulders, while they were chanting my name. I had a flashback to the day when I was on my father's shoulders watching the race in his little town. I was told that I had the eyes of a stallion and someone told me I was out of my mind.

It was true; I was somewhat out of my mind in that I was truly connected with my whole being the way I used to be as a child. Children also have the natural ability to think big. Don't be afraid to think big!

I won the race and ten years later, I'm still winning. I'm still winning because I have discovered the true power that we all embody. I have disciplined myself to only act on what feels good. When you, too, become connected to your essence, you will have the best tool available for true fulfillment right there in your body. You will be capable of creating, manifesting, and magnetizing amazing things.

I have developed a morning routine and do it ritualistically every day. You can do this too. Begin a ritual where you can ignite your day and open the doors of possibility. You are your best available tool. It's possible to carry the pure, magical, natural essence of childhood within your whole being while blending it with your language, creativity, and artistic expression.

You can unveil your potential as an individual. We can unveil our potential as a human collective.

Go down and go deep. It's in your nature. Descent with awareness becomes transcendence, and that's true fulfillment. My race had a finish line, but I realized along the way that there is no such thing as a finish. Nothing is finite.

Baby Steps

What better way to find true fulfillment than by the same kind of experience a baby has in taking his first steps!

I imagine myself as a baby. How joyous it was to take my first steps, make mistakes and fall. Not only that, but I know it was fun and joyous for my whole family to see me try to walk, to take that first step, to fall, and then, to get back up again.

Anyone who has watched a baby understands the joy of watching them take one step, then two steps, then three. They learn to walk, and eventually to run. The falling down along the way is part of the joy.

I still imagine myself having that essence. I am still a baby. I am still in the same body, and there is nothing that counts but taking that step. There is nothing else in my mind. A baby doesn't think about anything else but taking that step. When a baby sees somebody else run, they see possibility and not envy.

I still feel that joy in seeing others move and feel the wonder that comes with it. I still have that essence within me, and so do you. We lose contact with that essence because of how we have been conditioned in our adult lives. A baby step is a reminder of that.

One of my favorite quotes is this one, by Dr. Seuss: *Kid, you'll move mountains!*

This quote, from his 1990 book, *Oh, the Places You'll Go!* is a reminder that I am still a childlike essence, and I, too, am capable of moving mountains.

Conclusion

Do you set goals, but fall short?

Do you meet your goals, but when you arrive at your destination, feel unfulfilled?

Do you want to make authentic changes in your athletic performance?

Do you want to make authentic changes in your life?

With simple shifts in how you move, you can reconnect with your power through your body. You don't need special equipment. When you wake up in the morning, you already have everything you need to begin.

My story started with despair and failure, but led to the creation of a training method that has helped me and many others. My own journey landed me on the field of possibilities, where anything is possible. As evidence, consider that Spanish was my first language — I learned to read English from a classmate — and here I am writing a book that carries an authentic message for individual and world transformation. My SAT scores were way below average and my grades were subpar. I grew up in a low-income high-crime environment. I have gone from a survivor to a thriver! We all can.

You have read about the need to have *big visions* in this book. The creation of this book was actually one of my big visions and to produce the book, I followed the maxims of The Hart Method. I used the principles of the method to connect with myself, my body, my heart, and my vision, and this book revealed itself to me in a much more powerful way than I had foreseen.

I don't think this would have happened if I had written the book without using the method. I would have been stuck in the linear mentality you've read about in this book — point A to point B — and the book would have suffered. Instead, I kept my focus on the moment, on putting my foot down and staying connected to my authentic self. In doing so, I became a vessel that allowed this book to come through in the way it was supposed to come through, not for me alone, but for the whole world.

Do you have a big vision?

I deeply desire for individuals to connect with the intention of their vision. It's easy to start. Change how you walk, and I believe that can be the start to changing your life. Learn to drop your leg down toward the ground with awareness. That is the *ground maxim* of The Hart Method. As you have read, this is the starting point for coming into your power.

Be open to what life can bring you. True change starts with you. Through the maxims of The Hart Method, my hope is that you will reignite the joy that comes with movement, and the joy that comes with connecting to the natural power in your body. You will be able to carry this awareness over to your relationships, and create harmony in your life.

Go deep. It is the way to forward movement, fulfillment, and joy. It will be hard work, but the benefits are well worth it. You will be able to strip away the beliefs that have been holding you back, whether they are conscious or subconscious. Remember, you are not your beliefs. Putting the foot down is a reminder of that.

There is plenty of help around you. You just need to be open to connect with people who will help you look at yourself, your choices, and your ways of sabotage. Find people who know that your power lies within you and will help you to access it.

When you change your own world, you will be able to express that to others, and together, we will come to know that we are just one little part of this bigger thing that we call humanity. There is a connection between us; we are all in this together. True change is possible, not just by taking action or forcing change, but through connecting with your own body, your own self, and your own processes.

Whatever you are experiencing is the perfect starting point. You are ready now.

Your own individual life may be going through a void, or a darkness, but that is the perfect starting point. You are like an athlete going through a slump. It's what you do in that slump that is going to set up the next part of life. That is true of each and every individual life, and is also a reflection of the world.

How can we truly change as a world?

What are our goals as humanity?

How can we understand enough to fix the problems of the world?

We are all separate parts of humanity, but we are naturally connected in essence. We can find a way to reconnect to the whole despite our differences. Remember that we only have power and control over ourselves, but that is the key. Each individual can make a difference. The simple action of putting the foot down is the beginning of powerful change. One little simple and subtle shift in you can move mountains.

Forward movement is an inner job. You may be accustomed to forcing changes, but forced movements will be superficial and unfulfilling. They may give the appearance of speed and success, but this is an illusion. Authentic movement can't be forced.

Make the effort to go deep and connect with your body, and you will be able to move forward with joy. You may not always get the results that you were predicting — sometimes, the universe will move you in a different direction than you had envisioned — but you will have joy, health, and fulfillment, and you may well exceed your own expectations.

In the same way, when you connect with your inner self, your vision for your life may not be realized in exactly the way you predict, but you will certainly be igniting joy, happiness, and fulfillment.

Believe in the importance of thinking big but starting small. It starts with you. Come back to your body. Be aware of your movement. Descend back to yourself, and transcend to the field of possibilities.

It can start just by walking in a new way. Change the way you move, whether you walk, jog, sprint, skate, climb stairs, dribble, swing, jump, vault, or lunge. Change the way you get up in the morning. If you really want to see changes, change the way you move. Rebuild the harmonious bridge between your mind, body, and heart, and you will change your world.

Next Steps

Go to my website for your free download of my powerful The Hart Method Online Performance Kit program for athletes. Reach out to me for seminars, team trainings, personal training, speaking engagements, and possible collaborations.

Website: armandohart.com.

Like me on Facebook: Armando Hart@thehartmethod.

Follow me on Twitter: @Zeropointmethod.

Follow me on Instagram at: armando_hart.

About the Author

When we lose the powerful connection that exists between ourselves and our environment due to the stressors of life, Armando Hart believes that we can incorporate powerful change by moving our bodies with a deeper sense of freedom and joy, as we once did as a child.

After suffering a traumatic leg injury in 1996 that kept him sidelined at the Atlanta Olympic Games, Armando created a new training philosophy: *The Hart Method*. Armando's road to recovery made him aware of the connection between physical movement, environment, and life. The Hart Method of training maximizes this connection on all those levels. Now a world-class trainer, speaker, and mentor, Armando focuses on removing layers of social conditioning using movement. He works with professional athletes, fitness enthusiasts, and people at all fitness levels.

Armando grew up in Long Beach, California as a first generation Mexican-American, living in a low-income and high-crime environment. He became immersed in the mysterious and unique world of underground foot racing as an eleven-year-old boy. Armando had a taste of success and experienced the joy of running in this world, but he was continually challenged to find his own truth. He continued his underground running ventures until his early thirties. During this time, he was also involved in organized and sanctioned competitions — where he broke records as a sprinter — in races for the nation of Mexico, and while attending Cal State Long Beach.

Armando attributes the physical skills he possesses to the power of visualization in harmony with body movement. Although his Olympic dream was cut short, he believes that his dream of being a proponent of personal and world change is being actualized by once again embodying the maxims of his training system, The Hart Method.

Although his big vision is to bring joy and powerful change to the world, Armando believes that the change in the individual is much more effective in bringing forth world harmony. He believes we all have the ability and tools within us to make powerful change in our lives in spite of the challenges that surround us. They are available to us every morning upon awakening. He believes that true and powerful change starts with our body, our breath, our thought, and movement.

68766743R00098

Made in the USA
San Bernardino, CA
07 February 2018